THE 1910

SLOCUM MASSACRE

AN ACT OF GENOCIDE IN EAST TEXAS

E.R. BILLS

THE
History
PRESS

Published by The History Press
Charleston, SC 29403
www.historypress.net

Cover image: Watercolor study known as "A Human Skeleton." Rendered by English artist James Ward (October 23, 1769–November 17, 1859) with graphite, brown ink and brown and gray wash. *Image courtesy of Yale Center for British Art, Paul Mellon Collection.*

First published 2014
Second printing 2014

ISBN 978.1.62619.352.9

Library of Congress Cataloging-in-Publication Data

Bills, E. R.
The 1910 Slocum Massacre : an act of genocide in East Texas / E.R. Bills.
pages cm
Includes bibliographical references and index.
ISBN 978-1-54020-958-0
1. African Americans--Violence against--Texas--Slocum--History--20th century. 2. Slocum (Tex.)--Race relations--History--20th century. 3. Murder--Texas--Slocum--History--20th century. 4. Slocum (Tex.)--History--20th century. I. Title.
F394.S59B55 2014
976.4'229--dc23
2014010148

This book is dedicated to my father, Eddie Ray Bills Sr.

CONTENTS

PREFACE

In the present Convention, genocide means any of the following acts committed with intent to destroy, in whole or in part, a national, ethnical, racial or religious group, as such:

(a) Killing members of the group;

(b) Causing serious bodily or mental harm to members of the group;

(c) Deliberately inflicting on the group conditions of life calculated to bring about its physical destruction in whole or in part...

—Convention on the Prevention and Punishment of the Crime of Genocide, Adopted by Resolution 260 (III) A of the United Nations General Assembly on December 9, 1948, ratified by the United States on November 25, 1988

The Slocum Massacre began on a Thursday or Friday in late July 1910, sometime after an African American was slow to address a promissory note. Or when a Houston County road supervisor asked a black man to round up help for road maintenance. Or the second an aging boxer referred to as the "Great White Hope" was dispatched in Reno, Nevada. Or when Anderson County's vanquished, Confederate proud bitterly endured the policies of Reconstruction forty years prior.

Theories of origin abound, but the facts are clear.

White folks worked themselves into a panic and then a bloodlust. An untold number of black folks fled, disappeared and/or perished.

PREFACE

Some black folks retrieved and interred slaughtered loved ones while they hid or before they left. Some white folks slunk back to the scenes of bloody deeds and buried the evidence of their crimes by lantern light.

Many black folks abandoned the homes they had built and the land they owned and gave up the only lives they had ever known. Many white folks got away with murder.

ACKNOWLEDGEMENTS

Special thanks to Felix Green, Warren Pettinos, Maxine Session, Leigh Cravin, Linda Sue Stuard and the volunteers of the Houston County Historical Commission.

CHAPTER 1
SLOCUM MASSACRE

I

Palestine was startled early this morning by a rural telephone message from Slocum bringing information that a race war was on in that part of the country, and saying that fifteen negroes were killed there last night and six others this morning.
—Palestine Daily Herald, *Afternoon Edition, July 30, 1910*

On Friday, July 29, 1910, Anderson County sheriff William H. Black, of Palestine, received a trouble call at 11:00 p.m. It was John C. Lacy, sheriff of Houston County, immediately south of Anderson County.

Sheriff Lacy told Sheriff Black that a white man had killed two African Americans in Houston County, near the county line, and wondered if Black could meet him in Grapeland (in northern Houston County) to assist in the arrest. Some elements in both counties still hadn't come to terms with the idea that killing African Americans was against the law, so requesting backup in such cases was wise.

Sheriff Black informed Sheriff Lacy that he was busy, but he could break away if absolutely necessary. Sheriff Lacy told Sheriff Black not to worry about it and that he would attend to the matter himself.

At midnight, he called back.

During a preliminary investigation, Sheriff Lacy determined that the murders had occurred in Anderson County. Sheriff Black dispatched two deputy sheriffs forthwith.

The following morning, Sheriff Black traveled to southeastern Anderson County via horse-drawn carriage. He was thrown en route and significantly injured, but he continued on. When he arrived in the Slocum area, the local white community was in various stages of hysterics. "Everybody seemed to be almost scared to death," Black later recalled. "Everybody was armed with shotguns. They had the women and children all bunched up in places, and were guarding them. Many people were so scared and excited that they could hardly tell their own names."

In the days and weeks prior, a local African American businessman named Marsh Holley had gotten into a quarrel over a seventy-dollar promissory note with a handicapped white farmer named Reddin Alford.[1] It appears to have been a minor dispute, but there were hard feelings, and the prickly resolution became public knowledge. Also, a Houston County road maintenance supervisor had tasked an African American farmer named Abe Wilson to round up help for county road repairs. When a local white farmer named Jim Spurger[2] received word of Wilson's informal appointment, he was infuriated.

There was no evidence that Wilson ever actually approached Spurger, much less informed him his presence would be required on the county road repair crew; it was more a matter of southern white principle and racial hierarchy. The Confederacy was forty-five years departed, but broadly speaking, the Caucasian population of Texas did not consider African Americans their equals and went to great general, specific and systemic lengths to keep blacks second-class citizens in virtually every community (ergo black men did not tell white men it was time to help with county road maintenance).

When Spurger appeared at the site of the scheduled road improvements, he was carrying his shotgun. He later claimed he had brought it to go squirrel hunting on the way home. But instead of joining his fellow citizens in the road repair efforts, he flicked a dollar at the white county road overseer and said that he would not be working on county road details until a white man was appointed overseer. The white overseer no doubt regarded Spurger quizzically, and Wilson probably warily.

Spurger would later insist he received word that Wilson had muttered threateningly under his breath, but the claim was never substantiated.

Wilson's informal appointment to spread the word for the county road supervisor was clearly construed by Spurger as a violation of the "white" scheme of things in that part of the world, and once he took offense, he became a vociferous agitator. Holley's minor dispute with Alford grew major in association with Wilson's informal appointment, and

Caucasian indignation—stoked by Spurger—reinterpreted these events in predictable ways.

A black man tasked with informing his fellow citizens and neighbors that it was time to work on the county roads was suddenly a black overseer who was going to be in charge of white crews. A misunderstanding regarding a promissory note was now an "uppity Negro" trying to cheat a handicapped white man. Soon there were reports (all unsubstantiated) that African Americans in Anderson, Houston and Cherokee Counties were holding secret meetings and planning uprisings. Spurger and like-minded white folks even began claiming they had proof that a race riot was in the works.

II

The third and the most serious reason which is believed to be directly responsible for the tragedies is the seemingly baseless and unfounded wild reports and rumors which gained currency and which were magnified as they were repeated from mouth to mouth. These were to the effect that the negroes were preparing to rise and kill all of the white people.
—Dallas Morning News, *August 1, 1910*

One day earlier, Denson Springs (located a few miles east of Slocum) resident Art Harrison had telephoned folks in Elkhart (a larger community seven miles east of Slocum) and told them the "negroes of Cherokee and of this portion of Anderson County are assembling every night in large crowds and that some 200 had collected and he wanted to get enough white men to Denson Springs by sunrise to stop them." Sensing the urgency in Harrison's voice, the Elkhart telephone operator—anxious to help—offered to contact Palestine if more help was needed. Harrison indicated that such was the case.

Convinced—depending on the instigator or *carnage* barker—that they were under attack or about to be under attack, white citizens in the area armed themselves, called for help and began moving their families to churches and schoolhouses so they could be better protected. Smaller groups of men would guard the churches and schools, and larger groups would go on the offensive.

The calls for help brought white reinforcements from all over Anderson County; it seemed to be a summons for which a number of citizens had been waiting. They made stops at gun vendors and saloons and then headed south.

THE 1910 SLOCUM MASSACRE

When Anderson County district judge Benjamin Howard Gardner was informed of the impending bloodshed, he issued a court order closing every saloon and instructing hardware stores and other gun and ammunition vendors to cease and desist in the commerce of arms and munitions. But reports at the time suggested it was too late; several firearm suppliers had already sold out of ammunition. One man telephoned from Huntsville, inquiring about when and where he should report to join his white brethren. The local operator routed the call to the courthouse, and Judge Gardner advised the would-be lyncher to stay at home.

With their fears and prejudices roiled to a fever pitch, white folks in Anderson County manufactured an egregious, menacing foe; exaggerated minor frictions into full-blown malicious intent; and created a state of extreme animosity toward the local African American population—and an act of genocide began.

On Friday, July 29, just after sunup, three young black men set out to look after their family's livestock. Fifteen-year-old Charlie Wilson (son of Abe Wilson), eighteen-year-old Cleveland "Cleve" Larkin and eighteen-year-old Willustus "Lusk" Holley had spent the night at Wilson's grandmother's house near Sadler's Creek and left early, heading to Ava Wilson's (Charlie's mother) property less than a mile away. When they got about six hundred yards down the road, the young men spotted a group of six or seven armed white men, two of whom they recognized. At any other time, these black and white folks might have passed one another noncommittally, perhaps not friendly but not hostile either. But this time was different.

Without uttering a syllable, the white men raised their guns and fired on Wilson, Larkin and Holley, and Larkin was killed instantly. Wilson suffered thigh and ankle injuries and wounds to his chest, but he and Lusk managed to escape.

Larkin became the first casualty in what evolved into open season on African Americans in southeastern Anderson County (and, before it was over, northeastern Houston County).

A collection of white mobs made up of Slocum locals and heavily armed white residents from all over Anderson County roamed through the area in groups of six or seven or in mobs of thirty to forty and, according to some reports, up to two hundred. Members of the mobs engaged in what authorities later termed a "pot-shot" occasion, firing on black citizens at will. They moved from road to road and cabin to cabin, shooting down African Americans in their tracks.

AN ACT OF GENOCIDE IN EAST TEXAS

Sadler's Creek looking west off FM Road 2022. Like many creeks in the region, it was and is a marsh along some stretches. *Author's collection.*

Survivors of the bloodshed spread the word, and African Americans began fleeing. Their executioners were unmoved.

The white mobs followed blacks into the surrounding forests and marshes and shot many victims in the back as they fled. Several bodies were discovered with bundles of clothing and personal effects at their sides.

After surviving the first attempt on his life, Lusk Holley later joined his friends and neighbors in flight to Palestine. Accompanied by his older brother, Alex, and Willie Foreman, Lusk encountered a mob of eighteen to twenty white men (one on a horse) after crossing Ioni Creek about three and a half miles east of Slocum. The young men heard a man whistle, and the mob opened fire, killing Alex and wounding Lusk. Foreman ran for his life.

Lusk pretended to be dead as the mob inspected its work and passed on. As Lusk lay there with eight to ten buckshot in his lower left abdomen and a flesh wound in one arm, another smaller group of white men appeared. Lusk once again pretended to be dead. He recognized the voice of one prominent farmer, Jeff Wise, in the group as the men moved on. Wise was familiar with the Holley boys and commented that their deaths were a shame.

At some point on Friday, the few telephone lines that ran into the Slocum area were severed, and three additional casualties were reported in a black community at Squirrel Creek, three and a half miles northeast of Slocum. The white rampage went on until 10:00 or 11:00 p.m. that evening, when Sheriff Lacy was made aware of two of the early murders. From start to finish, the heavily armed white mobs went around murdering African Americans for approximately sixteen hours, but only five casualties were reported and only two were identified.

III

He told of a fierce manhunt in the woods, riddled bodies found on lonely roads and the spread of terror almost indescribable among the inhabitants of a very large area in the southeastern part of Anderson County.
—Galveston Daily News, *August 1, 1910*

On Saturday morning, the bloodshed started anew, but this time it was more intermittent and largely farther to the south, extending into Houston County.

When Sheriff Black set out for Slocum from Palestine at 10:00 a.m., he was followed by Godfrey Rees Fowler, a special deputy enlisted by Judge Gardner to assist in a grand jury investigation of the incident. Fowler was recently returned from military service in Nicaragua and was the grandson of Palestine's favorite son, John Henninger Reagan, former postmaster of the Confederacy.

The choice of Fowler for special deputy of the grand jury was at least a little curious. He was to some extent a war hero and, therefore, a good PR option, but choosing the grandson of a major figure in the Confederacy to investigate the murder of African Americans invited suspicion. The Daughters of the Confederacy had commissioned a Pompeo Coppini statue of Reagan for the city of Palestine just a few years earlier, and the city would establish a park for the statue just months after the Slocum Massacre. Fowler, however, had previously demonstrated himself to be committed to some modicum of duty and principle regardless of any possible personal biases.

While a Texas militia company commander stationed in Palestine before the outbreak of the Spanish-American War, Fowler and his men were ordered to the town of Henderson in Rusk County to protect an African American named Jim Buchanan. Buchanan was suspected of slaying a white family known as the Hicks (a husband, wife and daughter) in Nacogdoches County. Fowler's troops were part of a five-company contingent mustered by Governor Joseph Draper Sayers in October 1902. They faced a small mob in Henderson and turned it away. They moved Buchanan to a Rusk jail and had problems there, so they established a diversionary plan to ship him to Nacogdoches by train. The next day, mobs waited at stops between Rusk and Nacogdoches to seize Buchanan, but Fowler's company and the others transported him to Nacogdoches by horseback. When the Texas militia companies arrived in Nacogdoches with Buchanan, they were met by an armed mob of five thousand angry citizens. An October 16 headline in a Dallas newspaper known as the *Southern Mercury* indicated that Nacogdoches was "Fixed for a Barbecue" and that preparations had been made to "Roast Jim Buchanan, Negro Murderer."

Convicted murderer Jim Buchanan. In 1902, Texas militia transported him from Henderson to Nacogdoches for trial, foiling at least three lynch mobs en route. Company commander Godfrey Rees Fowler would later play a role in the investigation of the Slocum Massacre. *Galveston Daily News*, 1902.

The angry mob threatened and jeered the militiamen, and Fowler ordered his company to fixed bayonets, calmly leading his men to the county jail. When Fowler reached the front steps of the county jailhouse and the black suspect was delivered inside, he reportedly turned to the unruly mob and said, "You men can all go to hell. I'd like to see this nigger hung as much as you would, but you fellers are not going to hang him."

The following day, Buchanan was tried and convicted by a special term of the district court and sentenced to hang a month hence, on November 17. But the mob outside had grown so unruly, Buchanan—fearful of torture and/or the torch—waived the thirty days allowed to him by law and was hanged that same afternoon.[3]

Despite his family history, Fowler would not prove to be an agent for bigoted interests in the Slocum Massacre investigation proceedings. Early on, he rashly opined that he felt the mob of white murderers never comprised more than a dozen men (a claim supposedly based on the number of shots reported to have been heard during the carnage), but he, like Sheriff Black, was unwavering in his conclusion that the African Americans in the region had in no way, shape or form given their white counterparts the rationale for murder.

———

When Sheriff Black and Special Deputy Fowler arrived in the Slocum area, they discovered a terrified white populace, most of whom had slept overnight in churches and schoolhouses (if they slept at all). But it was increasingly apparent that the alleged African American mob that had supposedly conspired to attack the local white community hadn't materialized. In retrospect, this might have created more problems than it solved, especially for guilty whites.

First, if a mob of African Americans had attacked or had actually been preparing to attack, whites could have claimed self-defense and probably—*in that part of Texas in that day and age*—have justified preemptive slaughter. White families were still tucked away in guarded churches and schoolhouses; white folks had honestly expected conflict. With no attackers, they had no semblance of a rationale for the bloodshed the day before. The facts were damning.

Second, as previously stated, the African American community *did not* attack; the Anglo community—misled and suffering from a self-induced paranoia—*did*. At that time, blacks made up a large percent of the population of Anderson County and a substantial portion of the southeastern part of Anderson County. Would the groundless Friday night bloodshed compel the remaining African American population to do what their Caucasian neighbors had claimed they were planning to do all along? This was a legitimate white concern. What if the black citizens in southeastern Anderson County answered white savagery in kind?

And third, if the remaining African American community did not attack—couldn't attack or wouldn't attack—wouldn't their vestigial presence comprise a threat and serve as a constant source of uneasiness for the white community from that point forward? The remaining black community was witness and register to the white community's atrocities. For the moment (again, due to the day and age), African American narratives might not garner credibility or be treated seriously, but that might eventually change. Wouldn't it be better to be safe than sorry?

Regardless of what motive the local white population operated under, many seem to have decided to extend the previous day's rampage. By the time Black and Fowler were en route to Slocum, remnants of the Friday mobs were already at work south of there, effectively tying up (or eliminating) loose ends.

IV

Men were going about killing negroes as fast as they could find them, and so far as I was able to ascertain, without any real cause. These negroes have done no wrong that I could discover. There was just a hot-headed gang hunting them down and killing them. I don't know how many were in the mob, but I think there must have been 200 or 300. Some of them cut telephone wires. They hunted the negroes down like sheep.
—*Anderson County sheriff W.H. Black to the*
New York Times, *August 1, 1910*

Elkhart deputy sheriff Richard Stubblefield had planned to leave Elkhart not long after midnight on Friday night (after Sheriff Lacy had been in touch with Sheriff Black) to help investigate reports of trouble near Denson Springs, but he was warned that some of the local black men were lying in wait to assassinate him. He postponed his departure for a few hours to time his arrival in the trouble spots with sunrise, and he encountered no resistance or threats along the way. "Nowhere," he said, "could I find any sign of armed negroes." But this didn't stop the rumor mill. By the time Deputy Stubblefield reached the Slocum area, newspapers like the *Houston Chronicle* were already reporting him dead.

Black, Fowler and Stubblefield all encountered the same basic evidential status: numerous unarmed, *deceased* African Americans and hundreds of armed, *living* Caucasians. Black contacted Judge Gardner, and Gardner in turn contacted Adjutant General James Oscar Newton requesting assistance in the form of Texas Rangers and the state militia.

An African American known as John H. Hays was found dead in a roadway south of Slocum, alone when he was attacked or left by his companions when they fled.

An African American named Sam Baker was murdered at point-blank range at Dick Wilson's house a short distance from the Percilla and Grapeland Road. When forty-five-year-old Wilson, seventy-year-old Ben Dancer[4] and

A stretch of CR 1720 coming up on Silver Creek in the northeastern portion of Houston County. The landscape in several areas hasn't changed much since the Slocum Massacre. *Author's collection.*

eighteen-year-old Jeff Wilson (also African Americans) went to the house to sit with Baker's body, they, too, were gunned down on Wilson's front porch.[5] Their assailants, whom Mrs. George Scarborough[6] watched travel through her property and cut down some of her fencing, were identified as a group of forty to fifty white men, some on horseback.

After killing Dancer and the Wilsons on the front porch, members of the white mob dragged them inside and dumped their bodies in a hallway. Baker's body was found in a side room. He had been killed by a squirrel-shot shotgun blast at extremely close range. The hole in his chest was twice the size of a silver dollar.[7]

Across the Houston County line, just south of Percilla, a white mob reportedly decimated an entire black neighborhood that inhabited a mile-and-a-half stretch of dwellings along a county road (probably CR 1720 and onto CR 1725).

Before the bloodshed began, the long row of dwellings had been something of a day laborers' community that served local farms and

Downtown Palestine in the early twentieth century. *Courtesy of Palestine Public Library.*

merchants. If an establishment or spread needed help, it would come by the community in a wagon or buggy and pick up workers. The neighborhood was home to the laborers and their families and probably featured its own backwoods bustle, but on July 30, it fell silent. After a visit from a white mob, the sole remaining inhabitants were an old black couple, probably too proud, tired or debilitated to run. The gray-headed, white-bearded patriarch was reportedly shot dead in his rocking chair. His wife was slain in their doorway.

By Saturday afternoon, the phone lines to Slocum had been restored, but by then, most of the bloodshed was transpiring in Houston County. The churches and schools where white folks had braced for attacks were entirely unmolested, but the white bloodlust continued.

Meanwhile, problems were brewing farther north in Anderson County, particularly in Palestine. Several sources were mischaracterizing the trouble south as a "race riot," and the citizens of Palestine were afraid the violence might spread into the city. Fistfights began breaking out in the streets, and several nurses at a local hospital resigned their positions and left town to escape the approaching unrest.

A state militia from Marshall (helmed by Captain Will Lake and Lieutenant Colonel G.F. Rains) arrived in Anderson County at 7:25 p.m. They were soon joined by Texas Rangers E.L. Averitt, Thomas Brown, Sergeant J.L. Anders and Captain J.H. Rogers, all of Ranger Company C.

Though killing mobs were once again at work in both Anderson and Houston Counties from roughly sunup to sundown, only a handful of casualties were reported, the last two of whom were gunned down in a road near Percilla. They both had their knapsacks at their hips.

V

Following a call issued Sunday morning to citizens who reside between Slocum and Denson Springs, a dozen farmers and planters gathered at noon at Dick Willet's [Wilson's] farm, three miles southeast of Slocum, for the purpose of burying the bodies of those negroes that could be found. Willet's [Wilson's] farm was chosen on account of its central location and on account of the fact that four negroes were killed there. Scouting parties were dispatched through the woods and every little while a party would return bringing to the common cemetery the body of a dead negro.
　　　　　　　　　　　　　—Fort Worth Record, *August 1, 1910*

On Sunday, July 31, with militia and cavalry in place to preserve order, law enforcement officials performed a broader investigation of the lawlessness that had prevailed since Friday morning. When Sheriff Black's deputies had arrived Friday evening, they found no congregating (much less conspiring) African Americans. In fact, through Friday evening and into the morning on Saturday, the only living blacks they encountered were inside their homes, and the deputies were usually a welcome sight, invited in as protectors. There was absolutely no evidence supporting any aspect of a "Negro" plot against white citizens in the region.

Early that Sunday morning, Marsh Holley was discovered just south of Palestine on one of the roads leading into the city. For his own safety, he was taken to the county jail and locked up. He conveyed the massacre details of which he was aware but admitted they were mostly just hearsay. He also indicated that the promissory dispute between him and Reddin Alford had been blown out of proportion and was not the cause of the bloodshed.

Farther south, at Dick Wilson's place, a handful of black men began digging a trench twelve feet deep under the supervision of some of the Texas Rangers. Once complete, it became the final resting place of several unknown massacre victims. Reports listed the number of deceased occupants in the burial pit as six, four of whom were assumed to be Baker, Dancer and Dick and Jeff Wilson. This assumption was never officially confirmed, and the other two bodies in those reports went unidentified. The same reports stated that the bodies were wrapped in blankets and interred together in a large pine box. Other accounts said the bodies were unceremoniously dumped in the trench and suggest the exact number of corpses was unclear.

Some of the bodies were in various stages of decomposition, and a speedy burial as a matter of public health would not have been unheard of. A *Fort Worth Record* account indicates that before the informally scheduled mass burial took place, search parties combed the surrounding woods and thickets and periodically returned with additional bodies. On-the-spot inquests were performed by Alder Branch justice of the peace Byron Singletary.[8]

In retrospect, it's obviously probable that the mass grave at the Wilson place contained more than six bodies; there simply might have been only six identified or identifiable sets of remains.

In a different stretch of the sprawling crime scene, Anderson County deputy sheriff Riley Reeves and another officer known as Dunbar were reportedly accosted by a white mob of about seventy-five heavily armed men while attempting to transfer a group of living African Americans from one area to another. The mob demanded that one of the blacks be handed over, but Deputy Reeves refused, climbing on the wheel of his buggy and declaring that the "Negroes" were under his protection. Reeves told the mob that his passengers would be separated from him only over his dead body and urged the mob to disperse and go home. His bluff was effective, and the transport continued on.

At noon on Sunday, at least thirty African American women and children solicited direct help from the Texas Rangers, and the Rangers did what they could. When the killing had started and the women's husbands and brothers had been murdered or chased away, they gathered their children and sought refuge in a secluded cabin four miles from Slocum. When the carnage was over, they emerged shell-shocked, some widowed and some suddenly destitute.

As the day wore on, law enforcement officials established a headquarters at a farmhouse two miles southeast of Slocum. While attempting to gather witnesses and pursue arrests, they encountered repeated scenes of wholesale

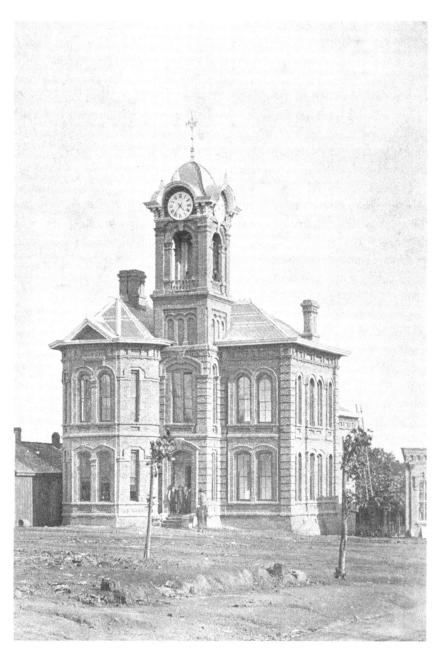

Anderson County Jail, circa 1900. Completed in 1880, it held several Slocum Massacre suspects as they awaited indictments and trial. It also simultaneously housed six African Americans waiting to testify against said suspects (placed there for their own protection). *Courtesy of Palestine Public Library.*

killing, horror and terrorism. One search party approached a one-room cabin in the forest and was startled when two adult African American men bolted out the back door and fled into the woods.

Inside the cabin, the search party found a terrified elderly black couple with five small children at their feet. On the only bed in the dwelling lay a late twenty-something-year-old black man, dead from a buckshot blast to his abdomen. The elderly couple said they had found him wounded on a nearby hillside the night before and had moved him into their cabin to help, but to no avail. The couple, the children and the two men who had fled had been holed up silently in the cabin for at least thirty-six hours with no food or water, tired, famished and unaware of the extent of the bloodshed that had occurred across the region, but well aware of the bloodshed that was transpiring in their corner of the woodlands.

When Special Deputy Fowler took grand jurors A.N. Starr and Gib Day and Justice of the Peace Singletary to investigate the Squirrel Creek community, which was usually heavily populated by African Americans, they discovered a ghost settlement now inhabited by only three blacks. A search curiously "failed to disclose any dead bodies."

The empty cabins in deserted African American communities were invariably riddled with marks of gunshots, and in one spot, as the *Dallas Morning News* put it, "a dead dog bore mute testimony to the tragedies."

In the late afternoon, Deputy Reeves and two Texas Rangers arrested Jim Spurger, Isom Garner, Walter Ferguson and Josh Bishop in the Slocum–Denson Springs area. None of the suspects resisted arrest, but Reeves later said he had been warned that he would be involuntarily relieved of his prisoners on the way to Palestine. Reeves and the Rangers headed north cautiously and delivered Spurger, Garner, Ferguson and Bishop to the county jail without incident at about 9:00 pm.

In the midst of law enforcement efforts to fix responsibility and apprehend the guilty parties, Sheriff Black issued a disturbing statement. "Men were going about and killing negroes as fast as they could find them," he said, "and, so far as I have been able to ascertain, without any real cause at all. These negroes have never done anything that I could discover. There was just a hot-headed gang hunting them down and killing them."

Black indicated that the "gang" or mob responsible for the mayhem probably numbered between two and three hundred and noted that eleven African American bodies had been found thus far. He estimated that the actual number of the dead was at least twice that many but ventured that determining the exact number of victims would be problematic.

"It is going to be difficult to find out just how many were killed," Black admitted, "because they got them scattered all over the woods. There will be some of them that won't be found until the buzzards find them."

CHAPTER 2
REGIONAL CONTEXT

I

The problem of the hour is not how to prevent lynching in the South, but the larger question: "How shall we destroy the crime which always has and always will provoke lynching?"

The answer which the mob returns to this vital question is already known. The mob answers it with the rope, the bullet, and sometimes, God save us, with the torch. And the mob is practical. Its theories are effective to a large degree. The mob today is the sternest, the strongest and the most effective restraint that the age holds for the control of criminal assault.

—Excerpt from "The Spirit of the South," an address delivered to the Mob Conference at Chatauqua, New York, by John Temple Graves on August 11, 1903, reprinted under "Defense of Lynching" headline in the Dallas Morning News, *August 12, 1903.*

Thursday, March 3, 1910, was supposed to go down in Dallas history as the day manned aviation was introduced to the city. Sponsored by the Dallas Chamber of Commerce and initially scheduled for late February, the event originally featured famous French aviator Louis Paulhan, but Paulhan was in a patent dispute with the Wright brothers, and the Wrights grounded him with a late court injunction.

His replacement, American daredevil Otto Brodie, showed up on March 2 and began preparing his Curtiss "aeroplane" for the following afternoon's rescheduled event at Fair Park.

The next day, however, Brodie and the chamber of commerce discovered that the debut of aviation in Dallas would receive second billing. The main event turned out to be a lynching.

A week before, Mrs. H.J. Huvens, of Pearl Street, noticed that her daughter, three-year-old Mary Ethel, was missing. She enlisted her African American maid, Flora Daingerfield, to help her find Mary Ethel, and Flora searched the house and then the barn. Flora found Mary Ethel in the barn with the Huvens family's black handyman, Allen Brooks. Flora grabbed Mary Ethel and rushed her into the Huvenses' house.

Mrs. Huvens contacted Dr. W.W. Brandou to examine Mary Ethel and make sure she was okay. Dr. Brandou vaguely indicated that the girl showed evidence of "brutal" treatment, and Brooks was immediately arrested and taken to the county jail.

Anticipating trouble, Dallas County sheriff Arthur Ledbetter transferred Brooks to the McKinney jail for safekeeping until his court date a week thence.

Ledbetter's instinct was correct. A mob of two to three hundred white folks—including Mary Ethel's father, H.J. Huvens—appeared at the county jail on the evening of Brooks's arrest and demanded he be handed over. Ledbetter informed the mob that Brooks wasn't there, but the boisterous throng didn't believe him.

Eventually, Ledbetter allowed Huvens and a lynch mob–appointed committee of six representatives to inspect the jail. They disappointedly confirmed that Brooks wasn't there.

The following week, after Brooks was snuck back into Dallas and smuggled into the county courthouse, the lynching delegation reappeared, this time thousands strong, including women and children. Court officials pleaded with the hellbent crowd, requesting that it allow justice to take its course, but appeals to reason only slowed the mob until more of its constituents fell in from local bars and saloons.

Before Brooks's court-appointed attorneys could even speak with him about his defense, the mob smashed all the glass out of the front courthouse doors and—despite six dozen police reinforcements—muscled its way in and interrupted Brooks's court proceedings on the second floor. The mob found Brooks under a table and took control of him.

The mob had its cohorts on the outside throw up a rope and then placed a noose around Brooks's neck. The throng outside jerked the defendant out of a courthouse window by his neck, and Brooks landed headfirst on the front steps. Several members of the mob proceeded to kick and stomp on him, but the fall had killed him or knocked him out, and he never regained consciousness.

The Old Dallas County Courthouse. On March 3, 1910, a lynch mob pulled an African American named Allen Brooks out of a second-floor window by a noose around his neck. *Author's collection.*

The mob fastened the rope to the back of a waiting vehicle, and Brooks was dragged to the intersection of Main and Akard Streets. There, he was hung from a telephone pole near the recently constructed Elks' Arch.

Dallas Police chief John Ryan arrived shortly thereafter and put an end to the proceeding, cutting Brooks down before the mob could burn his body. Onlookers fought over bits and pieces of Brooks's clothes and the hanging rope as mementos of the spectacle. Ryan took Brooks's body and ordered all the saloons in the area closed until the following day.

The mob, however, wasn't finished. Some of the leaders of the throng recalled that the Dallas County Jail had two other African American prisoners in custody and suggested that they deliver "justice" to them as well.

The mob turned toward the county jail, but once again, Sheriff Ledbetter was two steps ahead. By the time the mob (which had dwindled to six hundred men) reached the county jail, the two black prisoners, Burrell Oaks and Bud "Bubber" Robinson, were already en route to a Fort Worth jail via taxi. They were transferred again to Cleburne the next day.

This image of the Allen Brooks lynching on March 3, 1910, was made into a postcard, and participants mailed it to friends and loved ones across the region. *Courtesy of Texas/Dallas History and Archives Division, Dallas Public Library.*

The first aviation exhibition in Dallas history was witnessed by only a smattering of folks compared to the numbers that attended the Brooks lynching, but the occasion didn't go as planned anyway. The wind was up, and Brodie's aerial effects were underwhelming all around.

On March 4, the *Dallas Morning News* referred to Allen Brooks's murder as an "outbreak" of "popular passion," alternately trying to avoid offending critics and proponents of the lynching and ultimately blaming the court system (with which the lynch mob obviously interfered):

> *A newspaper which attempts to protest against such an exhibition of lawlessness as that witnessed in Dallas yesterday is not only embarrassed but disarmed at the very outset. If it would plead for the rights of the accused, it is silenced and shamed by the recital of a crime revolting beyond any power of description. If then it urges respect for law and order, it is promptly silenced by the reminder that the administration of law is often not only a farcical failure but a costly mockery of justice.*
>
> *There never was a mind powerful enough or subtle enough to justify lynching. It is in every case an irreparable hurt to society. But something may be said, in certain instances, not in justification, but in extenuation of*

the conduct of those who resort to lynching. Not every one who joins the mob is moved by a lust for bloodshed nor by a desire to witness the torture of a fiend. Many of them are moved by their contempt for the delays, reversals and failures of courts.

Of the 110 felony and 14 misdemeanor indictments for riot and lynching that a Dallas grand jury examined in regards to Allen Brooks's murder, none was deemed worthy of prosecution, and all were returned so as not "to incumber [*sic*] the court docket with cases of a doubtful or frivolous nature."

No family members came forward to claim Allen Brooks's body, and he was buried in a pauper's field. The only memorial he ever received was a picture postcard of the lynching that many citizens from Dallas mailed to their friends and relatives after the fact.

The Elks' Arch was eventually dismantled because of its association with the lynching.

Oaks[9] and Robinson, both charged with murder, were also hanged, but only after they had their days in court.

II

The press from all over the country is commenting unfavorably upon the actions of some of the citizens of Dallas of recent date. Murder, yes, lynching, is [a] crime to be condemned in the most stringent manner, and nothing, absolutely nothing, can be said in its defense. The sanctity of the home to our Southern citizens, however, is superior to the law. The people make the laws and the people can suspend the laws. And we notice that in the northern part of our free country they are suspended as much, if not more so, than in the southern part. Each section has conditions to contend with that can not be governed to suit the like or dislike of the other section. However human or inhuman they may be. The South is well able to take care of its own, notwithstanding the comments of our northern contemporaries.
—Jewish Herald *(Houston), March 17, 1910*

On Tuesday, April 5, 1910, one month after Allen Brooks was lynched in Dallas, Frank Bates was lynched forty miles southwest of Slocum in Centerville.

Like Palestine, Centerville was a county seat (Leon). Like the Slocum community, however, Centerville also had a considerable African American

Like Allen Brooks, Lige Daniels was a victim of summary justice at the hands of a white citizenry in East Texas. *Courtesy of Wikimedia Commons.*

population. In 1907, Centerville's black schools had 163 students (taught by 3 teachers), and its white schools had 92 pupils (taught by 2 teachers). A substantial portion of Leon County's population was black, but only white men were allowed to serve on Texas juries.

In December 1909, Frank and Dolly Bates were implicated in the death of Ben Moon near Marquez, three miles west of Centerville. In late March 1910, they were tried for Moon's murder, but the proceedings resulted in a hung jury even after two of the Bates associates turned state's evidence. Whether unsure they would receive a new hearing or fearful they would never get a fair trial under the circumstances, Frank and Dolly attempted to escape.

When Leon County deputy sheriff J. St. John entered their cell on the afternoon of April 5, he was reportedly pounced on by Dolly and thrown aside. In the ensuing struggle—and what was later described by newspapers as a "sensational" escape—St. John was shot in the mouth, and Frank and Dolly received flesh wounds as they subdued two other jailers. Their freedom was reportedly short-lived (some reports indicate they made it only one hundred yards before being caught), and they were returned to the Leon County jail before evening came.

That night, after it was reported that Deputy Sheriff St. John was near death, a local mob gained access to the county jail and lynched Frank and Dolly, hanging the former until his life was extinguished but cutting down the latter before his demise.

Authorities would later claim that someone had smuggled in a handgun to Frank and Dolly, but there was no mention of whom, and officials were (not surprisingly) unable to determine how members of the lynch mob obtained keys to the county jail.

There are apparently two J. St. Johns interred in the Centerville Cemetery: J.E. St. John (August 2, 1880–November 12, 1921) and J.F. St. John (August 8, 1861–April 1, 1937). Some newspapers of the day referred to Deputy Sheriff J. St. John's first name as "John," and others listed it as "Jeff." In either case, it appears Deputy Sheriff St. John was mistakenly reported to be near death.

Perhaps that's why Dolly Bates was spared.

III

Because innocent persons have been imprisoned under all forms of law, and even executed, we do not abolish law. Why, then, excoriate lynching for errors of rare occurrence? No human institution can be absolutely perfect; that is for God alone. But the white man of the South, and, for that matter, of the North, will submit to annihilation before they will tamely deliver over their helpless families to ravishment and murder.
—*Thomas M. Thorpe,* New York Times, *August 8, 1899*

On May 13, 1910, an African American named Dock McLane was lynched just north of Texarkana in Ashdown, Arkansas. McLane was accused of stabbing a white man named Ernest Hale and was originally placed in the

Bowie County jail. When officers attempted to transfer McLane to Ashdown, they were confronted by a mob of twenty-five white men and relieved of their suspect. When Deputy Sheriff Head tried to stop the mob, he was assaulted and severely injured.

The mob subsequently hanged McLane in the Ashdown jail yard. Hale recovered in a local hospital.

On May 14, an African American man named James Gozey walked into the Kirbyville Sheriff's Office (130 miles southeast of Slocum) and turned himself in. He confessed to killing James Snow near Ayers because he was afraid of being lynched. Whether he had actually killed Snow or leveraged a protected stay in a Kirbyville jail against certain death in rural Ayers is unclear. But the authorities in Kirbyville telegrammed the authorities in Mary, Louisiana, and Gozey was sent there so he might live long enough to receive due process of law.

On June 20, the body of a seventeen-year-old white girl named Maude Redding was found in a clump of bushes near Lone Star (forty miles northeast of Slocum) in Cherokee County. Her throat was reportedly slit from ear to ear, and her body was bruised and lacerated.

Maude's father (who was a constable) and brother had gone to Rusk on the day of the attack, and an African American convict known as Leonard Johnson was working off a fine on the Redding property doing plow work. Maude had left the Redding home for her customary one-and-a-half-mile walk to a music lesson in Lone Star and never arrived or returned.

Like Leonard Johnson, Jesse Washington was burned in public for the alleged murder and rape of a female relative of his white employer. *Courtesy of the Library of Congress.*

When Maude's body was discovered, Johnson was, as the *Palestine Daily Herald* put it, "immediately suspicioned and arrested."

Johnson "stoutly" proclaimed his innocence, but Cherokee County sheriff C.K. "Knox" Norwood and ten deputies took him into custody anyway. While en route to the county jail in Rusk, Sheriff Norwood and his men were accosted by an angry 150-person mob that encircled and overpowered them and then seized Johnson. When a number of African Americans in the area showed themselves disposed to defend Johnson against the mob, they were assaulted and beaten back.[10]

The mob tortured Johnson until he confessed and then hanged him, shot him and burned him at the stake.

The entire Lone Star community showed up for Maude Redding's funeral the following day, and Johnson's ashes were either raked into an unmarked grave or left to drift in the wind.

Sheriff Norwood later stated that not a single person in the lynching party was recognizable to him or his deputies, and his office would not be undertaking efforts to identify Johnson's executioners.

IV

If American women have any influence in the matter, why don't they use it to check lynching now? The answer is because they don't want to. It is mainly for their sakes that lynching takes place. It is on the bare, unsupported word of a woman—possibly an hysterical liar or a Potiphar's[11] wife—that a gang of cowardly desperados take the law into their own hands, and sometimes when a nigger is burned for an alleged attack on a woman it is the woman that sets him on fire.
—The Academy: A Weekly Review of Literature, Science and Art *(London), August 15, 1908*

On July 4, 1910, an African American transient reportedly walked into the Hub Bailey residence in Rodney (twenty miles south of Corsicana and seventy-five miles west of Slocum) at about 11:00 a.m. and seized Mrs. Bailey. Hub Bailey was in town at a store.

Mrs. Bailey tore herself loose from the transient, who allegedly brandished a razor, and ran into her yard screaming.[12] The intruder, frightened by her screams, also ran but apparently in the opposite direction. Mrs. Bailey suffered a severe cut on her arm, and the citizens of Rodney organized a posse to hunt down her African American attacker.

The posse hunted all day and late into the night, catching an African American near Coolidge at approximately 11:00 p.m. The posse returned to the Bailey household with the captured African American in the wee hours of the morning, and Mrs. Bailey reportedly identified him as her assailant.

The Rodney posse then transported the African American about four miles outside of town, near Eldorado, and hanged him from a tree at 7:00 a.m. on July 5.

The African American man's name was never established, and no one (including him) was ever charged or arrested for Mrs. Bailey's attack or the subsequent lynching. His death—like the deaths of Brooks, Bates and Johnson—was part of a pattern that had existed in Texas for decades.

According to an NAACP study entitled *Thirty Years of Lynching in the United States, 1889–1918* (published in April 1919), 335 lynchings were reported in Texas in that time period, and 78 percent of the victims were black. In other words, Texans lynched one person a month for thirty years, and almost 80 percent of the time the man or woman hanging on the end of a rope or smoldering in the remains of a fire was African American.

In every month for the six months leading up to the Slocum Massacre, an African American in the East Texas region was executed by a white mob based on allegation alone. No trials, no juries—simply white verdicts. And these injustices weren't exceptions to the rule; rather, they were the rule under which African Americans lived and died in that part of the world.

On the day an anonymous black transient allegedly intruded in the Bailey residence, however, a notorious black champion definitively intruded on white America's superiority complex.

V

In sections of the south the Jeffries and Johnson fight has taken on an aspect of seriousness, and some apprehension is felt in case the negro wins the fight. Public officials and congressmen from the south today confirmed the anxiety and some of the southerners say the ignorant negroes have begun to look upon the fight as a contest which will determine their position in social life.

—Palestine Daily Herald, *July 2, 1910*

In 1907, Robert Wilson Shufeldt Jr., osteologist, mycologist, museologist, ethnographer and white supremacist (among other things) published *The Negro: A Menace to American Civilization*. As one might deduce from the title, Shufeldt had little use for African Americans. At one point in the book, he plainly and unabashedly stated that "the negro has absolutely nothing in his organization that can be added to our own with the slightest value, while on the other hand, nearly everything about him, mentally, morally and physically, is undesirable in the highest degree." Shufeldt's racist manifesto would go on to be popular not just in the South but also across the nation.

Robert Wilson Shufeldt was an American scientist who harbored odious views on race and published two books on the subject: *The Negro: A Menace to American Civilization* (1907) and *America's Greatest Problem: The Negro* (1915). *Courtesy of Biodiversity Heritage Library.*

Meanwhile, Jack Johnson—an intelligent, well-spoken, physically graceful and powerful African American boxer from Galveston—was climbing brashly through the world heavyweight ranks. In July 1907, he knocked out former white heavyweight champion Bob Fitzsimmons in two rounds.

On December 26, 1908, Johnson defeated the reigning world heavyweight champion, a white Canadian named Tommy Burns, in Sydney, Australia, delivering a TKO in the fourteenth round. And if a black man taking the much-coveted world heavyweight boxing title weren't enough, Johnson also cavorted with white women (marrying three in his lifetime and having romantic involvements with several white female sex symbols, including Mae West, Lupe Velez, Mata Hari and Moulin Rouge star Mistinguett), cultivated a flamboyant lifestyle and enjoyed a life of cultural and material opulence.

Johnson was the antithesis of what black men in America had theretofore been permitted to be and what most of Caucasian America strove methodically to keep African Americans from being. After he defeated Burns, white animosity crystallized into an ethnocentric yearning (and subsequent

Jack Johnson—the son of freed slaves—was an African American fighter who became the first black world heavyweight boxing champion in 1908. His seven-year reign was a vexing affront to most Jim Crow–era whites. *The Life and Battles of Jack Johnson, Champion Pugilist of the World*, 1909.

search) for a "Great White Hope," a white champion who might restore the "natural" order of things.

As the world heavyweight champion, Johnson initially faced several white fighters whom promoters had billed as "Great White" hopes, but each proved to be more wishful thinking than serious contender. White yearning deepened, and eventually promoters convinced former legendary heavyweight champion Jim Jeffries to come out of retirement and challenge Johnson.

In his prime, Jeffries had been a great fighter, known for his strength, stamina and brutal left hook. He had never been knocked down, much less knocked out, and in his third fight, he knocked out a formidable African American boxer named Hank Griffin in the fourteenth round. Johnson had battled Griffin three times and never won.

In theory, white America had reason for hope in the Johnson-Jeffries matchup, but only in theory. Jeffries had been retired for five years and was one hundred pounds overweight. He had a small window to lose the weight and get back in shape at a moment when Johnson was in his prime. Hope sprang eternal nevertheless, and white America was optimistic.

Some folks—both white and black and paying more attention to the implications of the bout—were not at all optimistic and worried about the consequences of the match.

An editorial in the *New York Times* posited that the Johnson-Jeffries fight was a problematic proposition for African Americans: "If the black man wins, thousands and thousands of his ignorant brothers will misinterpret his victory as justifying claims to much more than mere physical equality with their white neighbors. If the negro loses, the members of his race will be taunted and irritated because of their champion's downfall."

E. L. BLACKSHEAR

Edward Blackshear, the first African American principal of Prairie View A&M, felt the "Fight of the Century" should be cancelled because it was exacerbating racial tensions in America. *Courtesy of the Special Collections/Archives Department of the John B. Coleman Library, Prairie View A&M University.*

THE 1910 SLOCUM MASSACRE

Edward Lavoisier Blackshear, the African American principal of Prairie View State Normal & Industrial College (now known as Prairie View A&M), northwest of Houston, was fearful and astute. He argued that what had come to be known as the "Fight of the Century" was increasing racial tensions that were "already stretched to a snapping point."

"If Johnson wins," Blackshear wrote, "the anti-negro sentiment will quickly and dangerously collect itself ready to strike back at any undue exhibition of rejoicing on the part of negroes. Race prejudice is already sufficiently acute in the United States. This fight ought to be called off."

If the fight had hazardous implications for African Americans in the United States in general, the dangers they posed in East Texas and, specifically, Anderson County were perhaps doubly or triply pronounced.

Many of Anderson County's white citizens had never completely overcome the bitterness and frustration they bore in the core of their very beings during Reconstruction. An Anderson County resident named Charles H. Moore recorded his thoughts and recollections on the subject in 1933:

> *Right after the war our country was placed under military rule, and was under the military until 1873. I was 14 years old then. The people during this time were supposed to have local self government, but the southern white people had no part in it, except those who turned renegade. The military arm of the government was there, I suppose, to keep down any local uprising among the southern whites, and to protect the negro. A short time after the surrender the carpet baggers came flocking into the south in droves. It was not long before they had all city, county and state offices in their hands, and in the hands of ignorant ex-slaves. The great majority of southern men were disenfranchised at the time. I do not think any county in any state of the south was cursed with a more dishonest and disreputable bunch of grafters than was Palestine and Anderson County. They put the negroes up to all kinds of deviltry, and promised them everything from social equality to 40 acres and a mule. The poor ignorant ex-slaves thought their days of labor were over, and that the Yankees would care and provide for them during the balance of their lives. Nearly all of them deserted their old homes and came to town so they could be in close contact and communication with their friends, the carpet baggers, who were running things to their own sweet desire. The negroes refused to work. Thieving and pilfering were rife. The civil courts refused to convict. They were in the hands of the negroes and the carpet baggers, and would not convict their friends. Sometimes the military arm of the government would step in and*

punish. I think the fairness and good judgment of the military commander, Capt. Hedbergh, prevented the wholesale sinking and destruction of the southern white people of our community. Conditions were awful. The southern whites were poverty stricken. Onerous taxes were placed on them. They were cowed, bled to death, desolated. The negroes were taught by the carpet baggers to be disrespectful. It was not safe, even in the daytime for a southern white woman to go anywhere without a male escort. No people in modern times, after a war, were ever called upon to face such conditions as were placed upon southern white people. Those in power in Washington and in the north at that time must have been bereft of all sense of fairness and humanity, or were ignorant of the conditions as they existed at that time, to have permitted a conquered people to suffer the wrongs heaped upon them during this period. Nothing like it would be permitted now. The world would rise in revolt. Hatreds engendered by war usually abate after the war is over, and the victor, proud of his laurels is willing to be a little magnanimous. But in this war the rule was reversed. If possible, the hatred of the abolitionist element of the north became more intense, the fires seemed to have been rekindled. They had placed the negro on a pedestal, and worshipped him. They saw a chance to destroy the white people of the south either by amalgamation or by utter destruction. No helping hand was ever extended to a southern white man or woman; no word of sympathy or encouragement was ever uttered. Instead, the very scum of the earth, the carpet baggers, were sent to the south to be their governors and masters. An attempt was made to enforce social equality between the negroes and whites. Can you imagine a more damnable thing ever entering a white man's head? Suppose they had been successful in this. Where would our nation be today? A nation of mulatoes.

A discomfort with, if not outright dislike for, African Americans seethed in the breasts of not all but many white Anderson County residents. By 1910, however, whites had for the most part managed to thwart the attempt "made to enforce social equality between the negroes and the whites" to which Moore alludes, thanks largely to the efforts of Special Deputy Godfrey Rees Fowler's grandfather, John H. Reagan.

Upon the cessation of the Civil War, Reagan, postmaster of the Confederacy, was imprisoned at Fort Warren on the twenty-eight-acre Georges Island at the entrance to Boston Harbor. While there, he closely followed the newspapers, paying special attention to events in the South and Texas and the corresponding responses to those events in the North.

John H. Reagan (circa 1890) was the postmaster of the Confederacy and a prominent nineteenth-century Texas politician. After the war, he advocated appeasing the Federal government so communities could be left to their own devices. *Courtesy of the Anderson County Historical Commission, Palestine, Texas.*

Reagan alertly surmised that if the white citizens of his home state could not master their hatred and vitriol toward the North, renounce slavery and their part in secession and commence in earnest to reconcile with the Union, they would suffer the twin calamities of prolonged Northern military rule and "universal negro suffrage." In his August 11, 1865 letter "To the People of Texas," Reagan stated the obvious but deeply offensive facts of the situation to the Lone Star body politic and public:

> *The State occupies the condition of a conquered nation. State government and State sovereignty are in abeyance, and will be so held until you adopt a government and policy acceptable to the conquerors. A refusal to accede to these conditions would only result in a prolongation of the time during which you will be deprived of a civil government of your own choice.*

Reagan then discussed their only realistic option:

> *The only wise and safe course for you to pursue is to accept promptly, unreservedly, and in good faith the terms and policy offered, and to go forward in the work of reorganization and restoration to the Union. This requires your assent to great pecuniary sacrifices, momentous changes in your social and industrial system, and a surrender of your opinions and prejudices on most important questions.*

And then Reagan addressed perhaps the chief suggestion of his entire correspondence:

> *To the conferring of the elective franchise on your former slaves, I anticipate stubborn and sincere opposition, based upon the ignorance of the great mass of them, and their total want of information and experience in matters of legislation, administration, and everything which pertains to the science of government, and upon the pride of race. And this objection may be sustained by pointing to the examples of Mexico, and the Central American and South American States, where by the enfranchisement of the Indians, and negroes, and all others, without reference to race or mental or moral fitness for the exercise of these responsible rights, they have been deprived of the blessings of peace, order, and good government, and involved in an almost uninterrupted series of wars and revolutions, often of the most cruel and barbarous character, for more than half a century, with no present prospect of an amelioration or improvement of their condition. But these difficulties are not insuperable, if you will meet them with patience and reason. I have no doubt that you can adopt a plan which will fully meet the demands of justice and fairness, and satisfy the Northern mind and the requirements of the Government, without endangering good government and repose of society.*

In pursuance of satisfying the "requirements of Government, without endangering good government," Reagan recommended "fixing an intellectual[13] and moral, and, if thought advisable, a property test, for the admission of all persons to the exercise of the elective franchise, without reference to race and color," well aware that the first and third fixes almost universally referenced race and color and disenfranchised the newly freed African Americans in the community. And in concluding the letter, Reagan openly acknowledged that "negroes will, it is hoped, gradually diffuse themselves among the greatly preponderating numbers of the whites, in the different States and Territories" and "many of them will probably go to Mexico, and other countries, in search of social equality."

Essentially, Reagan instructed his fellow Texans to recognize Northern authority and concede slavery in a timely manner so that they might go back to business as usual on many levels, specifically in terms of institutional racism and white control.

Interestingly enough, Texans and Texas politicians recoiled in horror at Reagan's suggestions of political expedience and, upon his return to Palestine, treated him like a traitor. The public and public office holders believed they could navigate the postwar era without drastic social or political changes and no official stance or acknowledgment of mea culpa, but their stubbornness was dashed by the Reconstruction Act of March 2, 1867, which officially replaced intransigent Southern state governments with military districts.

Suddenly, the heretical Reagan was proclaimed a sage and reenlisted by Southern Democrats to execute the practical suggestions of his open letter "To the People of Texas." In the end—and specifically over the next few decades—whites and white representatives in places like Anderson County were able to relegate African Americans to a socio-political substrata somewhere between slavery and second- or third-class citizenry and keep them there. The approaching "Fight of the Century" challenged a long-settled contest in the minds of most white folk; the Johnson-Jeffries bout would confirm or disturb the racial hierarchy that white bigots in Anderson County had labored steadfastly to reestablish and maintain.

VI

The greatest battle of the century was a monologue delivered to 20,000 spectators by a smiling negro, who was never in doubt and who was never serious for more than a moment at a time.
        —*Jack London*, New York Herald, *July 5, 1910*

Renowned author, journalist and social activist Jack London covered the "Fight of the Century" for the *New York Daily Herald*, and the *Dallas Morning News* published the *Herald*'s report of the event. London's lead paragraph said it all:

Once again has Jack Johnson sent down to defeat the chosen representative of the white race, this time the greatest of them. From the opening round to the closing round he never ceased from his witty sallies, his exchanges of repartee with his opponent's seconds and with the audience. And, for that matter, Johnson had a funny thing or two to say to Jeffries in every round.

Johnson, a son of American slaves, crushed America's "Great White Hope" and toyed with him (and it) in the process. Johnson stepped out of the ring

Instead of celebrating Galveston-born Jack Johnson's victory against Jim Jeffries in the "Fight of the Century," one cartoonist snidely depicted the African American population slighting Booker T. Washington in their newfound idolatry of Johnson. *Fort Worth Record*, July 7, 1910.

virtually without a scratch on him, and the "Great White Hope" had to be dragged to his corner, bloody, bruised and, as the *Fort Worth Record* phrased it, "dazed and incoherent."

In retrospect, it is impossible not to see Jeffries—who was not outwardly racist himself—as an unmistakable metaphorical representation of racist white America. And like the "Great White Hope" fans in attendance at the actual boxing venue, racist white America turned away from the result of the "Fight of the Century" "glum and silent."

But not for long.

In the aftermath, Blackshear's concerns were prescient. Riots broke out all over the nation.

A month after African American heavyweight boxing champion Jack Johnson dismantled the "Great White Hope," images of the contest were still forbidden in most parts of America. *Commerce Journal*, August 5, 1910.

In Chicago, a group of white patrons left a saloon shouting, "Let's kill the first nigger we see!" They promptly pulled the first African American they spotted off a passing trolley and proceeded to kick and beat him. Fortunately, they were stopped by the police.

Three black men were killed at a riot in Uvaldia, Georgia. A white deputy sheriff was killed while trying to calm black revelers in Mounds, Illinois. Two black celebrators were killed in Little Rock. Police in St. Louis clubbed a black mob into submission. "Noses were made bloody and heads were cracked" when whites tried to disperse a victory celebration parade of blacks in Columbus, Ohio. And several African Americans in Houston were assaulted within an hour of the Johnson-Jeffries fight result.

There were serious disturbances reported in dozens of communities across the country, including New York, Philadelphia, Pittsburgh, Kansas City, Atlanta, Charleston, Springfield, Joplin, Fort Worth, Tyler and elsewhere.

No trouble related to the "Great White Hope's" defeat was reported in Palestine or Anderson County, perhaps because African Americans there knew better than to openly gloat or celebrate. The July 4 afternoon edition of the *Palestine Daily Herald* featured a headline that noted, "Johnson Wins in the 15th Round," but curiously featured a half-page photo of Jeffries instead of Johnson above an article celebrating the former's most important fights.

By July 6, the four-million-member United Societies of the Christian Endeavorers and several police chief associations were leading a nationwide movement to prohibit exhibitions of pictures or film footage from the Johnson-Jeffries fight. And Texas governor Thomas M. Campbell (a Palestine native) was quick to join the effort, indicating that he would ask representatives participating in the approaching special session of the state legislature to craft a law banning the display of images from the "Fight of the Century."

The leaders from most other states agreed with the ban, but there were some notable exceptions, including the state of Utah and the cities of New Orleans, Philadelphia and New York. New Orleans decided to allow the pictures to be displayed but ordered that African Americans not be permitted to "mingle" with whites in theaters where the images were presented. New York City mayor William J. Gaynor and Philadelphia mayor John E. Reyburn imposed no restrictions on the images whatsoever.

CHAPTER 3

MEDIA RESPONSE

I

Inasmuch as many outrageous reports have appeared in the papers over the country concerning an alleged race war in and around Palestine, reports that were and are utterly at variance with truth and veracity, doing the name of Palestine and Anderson County, and the inhabitants thereof, a very great injustice, and which constitute a slander on this people, and since these reports have been extensively printed under a Palestine dateline, and yet showing on their face that they were not written in nor sent from this city because of their distorted statements, statements showing that the writers not in the least familiar with this section's conditions, we deem it our privilege and our right to make a statement of what actually did happen and request that you give it all publicity in your columns. We ask this as a privilege of fair treatment.

—First paragraph of action statement, Palestine Board of Trade,
Palestine Daily Herald, *August 3, 1910*

In the August 3 edition of the *Palestine Daily Herald*, the Palestine Board of Trade denounced the exaggerations and mischaracterizations rampant in the reporting of the "Slocum affair," particularly as they portrayed the city of Palestine and Anderson County, in general, in an unfavorable light.

The board had met the night before and established a three-man committee composed of some of Palestine's most affluent sons (H.V. Hamilton, A.B. Hodges and B.F. Rogers). The board assigned them the charge of preparing a statement aimed at unsullying the city's image.

To be fair, the *Herald's* coverage of the event was more accurate than that of most other newspapers inside and outside the state. Its first headline on July 30—before anyone really knew the extent of the bloodshed or had established the motives behind it—was cautious. It stated, "Whites and Negroes in Serious Conflict." Obviously, the term "conflict" implies two committed parties at variance or in opposition, and it would later become clear that there had been only one. But on July 30, rumors still had white folks thinking they might at any time come under attack, and most legitimately believed they were involved in a conflict.

Two other Texas newspapers reported on the massacre on July 30. The *El Paso Herald* announced, "Ten Negroes Are Killed in Texas Race Riots" in a banner larger than the newspaper's masthead. The *Fort Worth Star-Telegram* featured a banner that read, "Many Killed in Serious Race Riots in Eastern Texas." Both publications intentionally or unintentionally sensationalized the story, and their mischaracterizations would become progenitors for a categorically misleading strain of reporting.

On July 31, the *New York Times* headline, "Score of Negroes Killed by Whites," was an exception—it approached the truth. But virtually every other publication would injudiciously go with something resembling the *Herald's* or the *Star-Telegram's* July 30 lead.

The *Dallas Morning News* headline proclaimed an "East Texas Race Riot; Eighteen Negroes Killed." The *Greensville Morning Herald* headline read, "Race Riot: Bloodshed." The *Fort Worth Record* alleged a "Bloody Race War." The *Galveston Daily News* reported a "clash" between whites and blacks that was the result of a raging race riot. The *New York Tribune* announced that "Fifty May Be Dead in Texas Race Riots," and the *Star-Telegram* doubled down, upgrading the previous day's "race riot" to an all-out "East Texas Race War."

The July 31 edition of the *Abilene Daily Reporter* would portray the trouble in Anderson County as a "race riot," but also betray a blatant bias. The second deck stated that "Negroes Are Armed and in a Bunch," and the third deck noted that "Whites Gathered Arms and Went Coon Hunting."

The early reporting clearly bothered the business set in Palestine, but it also riled racist factions in communities across the region. Phrasing the situation in Anderson County as a "race riot" basically suggested to many

AN ACT OF GENOCIDE IN EAST TEXAS

ABILENE DAILY REPORTER

VOLUME XIV — ABILENE, TEXAS, SUNRDAY, JULY 31, 1910 — NUMBER 322

RACE RIOT AT SLOCUM RESULTS IN DEATH OF 23 NEGROES, 4 WHITES

FIERCE FIGHT STARTED IN QUARREL OVER SMALL DEBT.

NEGROES ARE ARMED AND IN A BUNCH

Whites Gathered Arms and Went Coon Hunting--The State Militia Ordered To Scene at Once

NEGRO USED GUN; SHOT WHITE MAN

CO. DEMOCRATS MET SATURDAY

TRAVELING MEN BEAT ATHLETICS

CONVENTIONS HELD BY THE DEMOCRATS

Like most of the newspapers that ran stories on the Slocum Massacre, the July 31, 1910 edition of the *Abilene Daily Reporter* mischaracterized the incident as a "race riot" instigated by troublemaking "Negroes." Unlike most publications, however, the *Reporter* blatantly conveyed its bias with the first phrase of the final subhead: "Whites Gathered Arms and Went Coon Hunting." *Courtesy of the Abilene Public Library.*

51

whites that the African Americans there were out of control. In most communities, the collective white male psyche would have deemed this unacceptable and, more often than whites like to admit, would have justified any manner of violence under the circumstances. African American writer, attorney and former Palestine resident Leigh Cravin addressed this issue in a 2011 editorial:

> *There have been hundreds of other Slocum-type incidents all across America throughout history where thousands of blacks have been slaughtered at the hands of hate-filled mobs of whites. In almost every case the media has characterized the resulting white violence as the result of a "race riot." The same "race riot" media characterization of the brutal massacre of one of my grandfathers, as well as thousands of other innocent blacks, has served only one purpose and that is to cast the aura of blame onto innocent black individuals and to let brutal white criminals go free.*

The grandfather Cravin referred to was killed during the Slocum Massacre, gunned down in cold blood while he was trying to take cover in his bedroom.

———————

As word of the Anderson County "race riot" spread, violence followed.

On the evening of July 30, at approximately seven o'clock—not long after the *Star-Telegram* reported serious "Race Riots in Eastern Texas"—an African American named Isaac Sims accidentally bumped into a white man outside a movie theater in Fort Worth. The white man unhesitatingly struck him in the jaw, knocking him to the pavement.[14]

When Simms attempted to regain his feet, the white man struck him down again. Then, when Simms accordingly lost "his sense of better judgment" (as reported by the *Star-Telegram*) and made a "movement of retaliation," another white man in the vicinity shouted, "Look at the nigger! Look what he's doing."

Simms turned and ran toward the Fort Worth Police Department, and several enraged white men followed in pursuit.

As Simms neared the entrance to the police station, a member of the mob chasing him (which had grown to almost one thousand) tripped him, and he fell to the pavement. At that point, two members of the Fort Worth Police Department rushed out and rescued Simms from the surrounding mob and probably thwarted a lynching.

II

The facts are these, without color: On Friday, July 30th, just passed, a community disturbance occurred at Slocum, a small country neighborhood, in the extreme southeastern part of this, Anderson County, about fifteen miles distant. In which some ten negroes were killed by white men presumably, the result, according to the best of the information, of a series of rumors in effect that the negroes of the community had on hand a plot to raid the homes of the white people of the community and kill the members of the white homes, rumors neither confirmed nor disproved.

—Second paragraph of action statement, Palestine Board of Trade,
Palestine Daily Herald, *August 3, 1910*

The second paragraph of the Palestine Board of Trade's action statement was loosely observant of the facts. Rumors regarding African American plans to kill white people had already been addressed and dismissed by leading law enforcement officials, including Sheriff Black and Special Deputy Fowler. Proffering the notion that the rumors held any credence was an exercise in selective ignorance or premeditated spin. The "Slocum affair" was a public relations nightmare, and Palestine officials obviously tried to mitigate the damage.

By July 31, the details of the bloodshed had begun to take on a life of their own. In some cities, the facts were manipulated to sell newspapers, and in one city, they were twisted to swell racial pride.

East Texas native Bessie Coleman was the first African American female pilot and the first person of African American descent to hold an international pilot's license—but she was able to achieve these distinctions only after she escaped Jim Crow Texas. *Courtesy of the National Air and Space Museum.*

THE 1910 SLOCUM MASSACRE

The African American–owned and operated *Chicago Defender* (published by Robert Sengstacke Abbott) took the unfounded "black attack" rumors and enlarged on them. The *Defender*—whose motto was (and still is) "If You See It in the Defender, It's So"—introduced an August 6 headline that stated, "200 Whites Killed and Many Wounded in Race War in Texas" and ran a second deck that stated, "Only a Lack of Ammunition Forced Negroes to Surrender." In the black *Defender*, false white rumors were simply given license:

> *The white had been so cruel in their treatment towards the Negroes that it became unbearable. They* [the Negroes] *were forced to protect themselves, they organized 300 strong and demanded to be let alone and treated as peaceful citizens. The whites had started what they called a war of extermination and the fight was on. These sturdy farm hands proved to be real men and it would have been the extermination of the domineering whites had not the state militia been called out,* [and] *of course they joined their brethren, the white. Then the Negroes gave them a taste of what a black man can do when goaded to it; they fought a pitched battle, 300 Negroes against 1,500 whites. The negroes entrenched themselves and 15,000 could not have taken those entrenchments had their ammunition not have gave out, and even then the single ones among them held the works until the married men had made good their retreat. Then and not till then did they surrender. Thus proving their unflinching manhood, and loyalty when the test was made. The estimate loss of whites killed and fatally wounded reached the 200 mark while the Negroes lost but 30 all told. Those taken prisoners were 120 single men, the others are free, thanks to the willing sacrifice of their comrades. We are all awaiting the fate of those captured in this land of barbarians of ancient days.*[15]

In the "land of barbarians of ancient days," the fanciful and frenetic press coverage of the massacre was bad for Palestine, and there were indications that forces in the community tried to downplay the seriousness or severity of the actual circumstances. The *Palestine Daily Herald* was one of the more reliable sources on the Slocum Massacre early on but became less so in the aftermath. This was perhaps understandable from a short-term, white point of view, but in the long run, it only clouded the truth. The facts were too consequential to remain obscured.

CHAPTER 4

INDICTMENTS

I

The women of Tyler are sending flowers by the wagon load to the men in jail awaiting trial on a charge of lynching the negro, Jim Hodges. Jim Hodges may have been innocent, those women don't stop to investigate, but they look upon the lynchers as their protectors from the most horrible fate that can befall a woman, and honor them accordingly.
—Bryan Daily Eagle and Pilot, *May 15, 1909*

On April 30, 1909, at approximately 8:00 p.m., an eighteen-year-old white girl named Winnie Harmon was allegedly beaten and left in a barn just outside Tyler with her hands tied behind her back. Her brother discovered her a short time later, and her attacker was described as an African American man with atypically dark skin, dressed in blue coveralls and a black shirt.

Smith County sheriff Wig Smith formed a posse and found a dark-skinned black man named Jim Hodges at another African American's house the same night, four and a half miles outside Tyler. When the posse tried to arrest Hodges, an older black man at the residence protested and threw an axe at Sheriff Smith—*twice*.

The elder African American's attempt to thwart Hodges's arrest was incredible and clearly unimaginable in that day and age, but the posse was undeterred. It took custody of Hodges and transported him to the Smith County jail. The elder African American doesn't appear to have been arrested or retaliated against, almost as if members of the posse knew they were on an insidious errand and didn't want the treachery of the task to be any more pronounced than it already was.

When Hodges was presented to Harmon the next morning for a positive ID, Harmon reportedly couldn't be sure he was her attacker.

"I can't tell," she said. "I can't say he is the negro, but I can't say he is not the negro."

Unfortunately, many citizens of Tyler subscribed to the *guilty until proven innocent* philosophy where African Americans were concerned. At approximately 11:15 a.m., a white mob three to four thousand strong broke into the county jail and seized Hodges.

The lynch mob transported Hodges to the site of the new Smith County Courthouse, which was then under construction. A few members threw a rope up over an enormous derrick—which was being utilized at the site for hoisting large stones for the new courthouse—and fashioned a noose on one end, placing it around Hodges's neck. Several men then took hold of the other end and, with one simultaneous pull, jerked Hodges up into the sky.

Hodges squirmed as he swung back and forth high above the mob, and then his movements dwindled to a twitch or two before he grew still. Within ten minutes, the construction site was empty, save the deceased, whose gruesome figure hung motionless in midair.

No one involved in the crime even attempted to conceal his identity. As the May 7, 1909 edition of the *Alto Herald* put it, "Those who took part in the lynching went about it just as they went about their daily business."

By the time Governor Campbell received word of the Hodges lynching, it was too late, but he immediately dispatched state militia to Tyler. On May 3, state legislator Chester H. Terrell (of San Antonio) introduced a House resolution calling on the governor to submit a measure that required the criminal district court of Smith County to indict those involved in the affair, and though Terrell's measure was immediately buried in committee (and never revisited), there was an earnest attempt to prosecute the Hodges lynching. District court judge R.W. Simpson, Sheriff Smith and county attorney Roy Butler conferred, and over a dozen arrest warrants were issued.

Butler stated that the evidence he had accumulated thus far did not demonstrate Hodges's guilt and that the wrong party appeared to have been executed. Winnie's father, M.J. Harmon, had been present when the white mob stormed the county jail and tried to dissuade members of the mob from taking the law into their own hands, but with no success. And all this while

Not every African American lynching victim was male. On May 25, 1911, Laura Nelson was lynched alongside her teenage son, L.D., near Okemah, Oklahoma. *Courtesy of Wikimedia Commons.*

Winnie was fairly recovered, apparently not having been seriously harmed to begin with.

On May 6, the names of the alleged lynchers were released. They were: Lewis Adams, Horace Austin, R.E. Bryan, Audrey Campbell, Ross Ford, Ed Francis, Lewis Francis, Will Griffin Sr., H.F. Lindley, Joe Mattesota, Henry Paybrook, Birdo Pyron, J.D. Sullivan, Horace Turner, Walter Turner and John Wilkerson. Judge Simpson immediately began examining witnesses to secure grand jury indictments.

On May 13, Judge Simpson discharged R.E. Bryan and Audry Campbell, and Lewis Adams, Ross Ford and Horace Turner were granted bail at $5,000 each. H.F. Lindley, Joe Mattesota, Lewis Francis, Horace Austin, Birdo Pyron and Henry Paybrook were held without bail.

When Texas Ranger captain J.H. Rogers (the same captain who would go on to lead the Ranger effort in Anderson County) appeared outside the courthouse with the prisoners, the crowd that had gathered greeted him and his men with jeers and contempt, expressed with enough animosity that Captain Rogers had his men draw their revolvers and fire two shots in the air as they approached the Smith County jail. The trial date for the accused was scheduled for the next term of the district court, which was slated to commence on June 21.

Meanwhile, Judge Simpson was not comfortable with the general public's disdain for the charges against the lynchers and, what's more, held some of the more powerful, propertied elements of the community responsible. In his preliminary remarks, he made it clear that he would "gladly make any sacrifice if it would recall the flagrant and uncalled for violation of the law in Tyler on May 1, when the law was trampled upon and brought into disrepute by the very class of people who need the law for the protection of their wives and property more than any other class.

"If the administration of the law in Smith County does not suit the wealthy," Simpson continued,

> *they can go to other places, but when you and I disregard the law and bring it into disrepute we do an irreparable injury to ourselves and our posterity, and I give notice now that any crowd which by mob violence overrides the law while I am judge of this district may expect me to do my whole duty in seeing that they are brought to justice. I am satisfied that men were implicated in this unfortunate affair besides those men arraigned here and it is to be regretted that all alike could not have been brought to justice.*

On July 1, after a special eight-day session that included incriminating eyewitness testimony from a Smith County deputy sheriff, the all-white grand jury returned a no bill, concluding that the criminal charges alleged in the indictments were not sufficiently supported by the evidence. The grand jury proceedings were adjourned, and the imprisoned members of the lynch mob were released.

The cruel injustice of the Jim Hodges's lynching—magnified by the obvious, blatant disregard for the facts that led to it—was never sufficiently addressed, resolved or answered for.

II

Why are there so many lynchings? Because the law does not attend to its business properly. If our people could rely on summary justice being meted out to murderers and their like, there would be no need for lynchings and there would be none. To our courts in their laxity and looseness of procedure are chargeable the lynchings of our land and the excess of our murders.
—Greenville Morning Herald, *December 7, 1910*[16]

When the *Athens Review* and *Palestine Daily Visitor* newspapers in Anderson County published editorials that sympathized with the white mob that lynched Jim Hodges in Tyler, Anderson County district court judge Benjamin H. Gardner—concerned that affirming mob violence in the Hodges case might lead to more lynchings in the area—issued "A Word of Warning" in the July 10, 1909 edition of the *Palestine Daily Herald*:

I want to say to you gentleman, and I want to say it so that it can be spread all over this district, that I regard such stuff as rot. I regard it as anarchy, and all threats, political and otherwise, to deter an officer from his duty should have no effect whatever. I say to you that so long as I am judge expect to follow the law and I do not purpose to set it aside to please any mob or any crowd of people. I am saying this, not because there is an emergency now, but as a matter of warning. I want everybody in the county to understand that the judge in this district is not going to tolerate mobs and mob violence for one moment. I say to the sheriffs in this district, and I believe they will do it, that whenever a mob undertakes to take a prisoner away from them, they should, if necessary, shoot, and shoot to kill. I believe there is no more cowardly thing than for a sheriff to surrender to a mob. I believe, furthermore, that a mob is a natural coward. There is no bravery about it. There is bloodthirstiness—there is a desire to take someone's life—but whenever they know that a sheriff is at the helm that will shoot, the mob is going to slink off like a coward.

Judge Gardner indicated that he would not tolerate Anderson County law enforcement officers who wavered in the face of a mob or jury commissions that advocated or sympathized with mob violence of any kind or seated grand jurists who advocated or sympathized with mob violence of any kind. Then, Gardner concluded by stating that if his critics didn't like his stance on mob violence, they were free to organize a political machine and put him out of office. "I do not want to hold office over people who would have me to connive or wink at any kind of mob violence," he said.

Judge Gardner's bold stance was applauded by the July 1, 1909 edition of the *Houston Daily Post*. The *Post* posited that Judge Gardner's "courageous expressions from the bench" could not be reiterated too often:

The South needs brave judges and brave officers who will never swerve from the line of duty in the face of a mob. We know the futility of convicting the members of a mob in most cases, so the best way to deal with the question is for the officers to prevent the lynching beforehand...

A lynching is a disgrace to any community where it occurs, it is a disgrace to the State in which it is committed and a disgrace to the country as well. The evil is as prevalent in the South as ever because in too many instances the officers do not take such

Judge B.H. Gardner served as the Fourth District Court judge for Anderson, Henderson and Houston Counties from 1904 to 1912 and made every effort to prosecute the parties responsible for the Slocum Massacre. *A Centennial History of Anderson County Texas*, 1936.

precautions as are necessary to prevent it. Some officers do not realize that no greater testimony of their inefficiency could be given than the lynching of a prisoner in their custody.

In mid- to late 1909, it might have appeared that the critical light shone on lynching by Judge Simpson's and others' attempts to prosecute it would make the general public indignant enough to consider lynching anathema, but as earlier chapters have shown, such was not the case. As previously noted, in every month leading up to the Slocum Massacre, there were typical and high-profile lynchings in the region, and just over a year after Judge Simpson's attempt to bring Jim Hodges's murderers to justice in Tyler was deplorably abridged, Judge Gardner's convictions on the subject would be tested.

III

The slaughtering of what most of us around Palestine think to be innocent negroes was done by a white riff-raff, and every effort is being made to apprehend the guilty parties.
> —*J.F. Weeks, Palestine attorney*, Houston Chronicle,
> *August 2, 1910*

The July 1910 action reports for Texas Rangers, Company C, indicate that Ranger sergeant J.L. Anders arrested three men—Josh Bishop, Isom Garner and Walter Ferguson—on the suspicion of murder in the Slocum–Denson Springs area of Anderson County on July 31. Contemporary newspaper accounts also reported the apprehension of Jim Spurger, who was probably taken into custody by Anderson County deputy Riley Reeves.

The August 1910 action reports for Texas Rangers, Company C, start on August 1 with the arrests of G.W. Bailey, Morgan Henry and Frank Bridges, all charged with murder, the first two apprehended by Sergeant Anders in Palestine and the last arrested by Ranger Averitt in Slocum. Houston County sheriff Lacy also arrested Andrew Kirkwood and B.J. Jenkins and placed them in the Crockett jail, later transferring them to Palestine.

The previous afternoon, Anderson County sheriff W.H. Black had stated that it would be virtually impossible to determine how many African Americans had perished in the two- to three-day reign of killing, and at some point, Judge

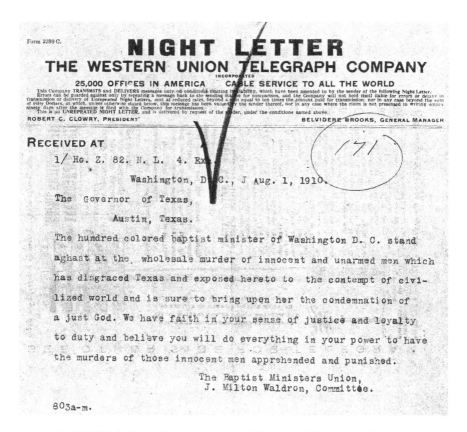

August 1, 1910 "Night Letter" (telegram) from influential African American minister J. Milton Waldron to Texas governor Thomas M. Campbell. *Courtesy of Texas State Library and Archives.*

Gardner determined that the lack of an accurate number of victims should not impede a county attempt to seek justice. On Sunday evening, July 31, he told the *Fort Worth Star-Telegram* that his duty was not to "find out how many negroes were slain, but to bring to account those guilty of the killings."

The *Star-Telegram* also reported that while most of the African American casualties came at the hands of the white mobs during the massacre, some also perished from mistaken fire.

When law enforcement officials—who were all white—finally arrived in remote trouble areas, some of the surviving African Americans understandably mistook them for remnants of the murderous mobs and reacted with panic, terror and, in some cases, threatening stances of self-defense; this presumably led to some of their deaths.

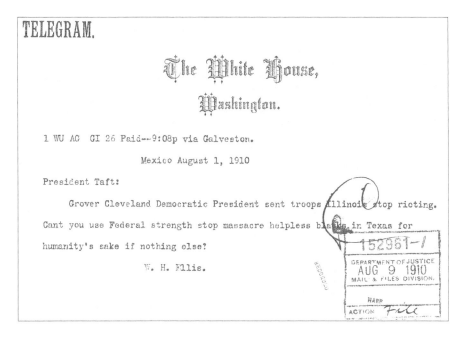

August 1, 1910 telegram from successful African American entrepreneur W.H. Ellis to President William H. Taft. Ellis, a Victoria native, was known for his advocacy of the black emigration movement in the late nineteenth century. *Courtesy of the National Archives & Records Administration, College Park, Maryland.*

Accounts provided by the chief investigators of the incident indicated that though only a half dozen victims had been officially identified, up to two dozen African Americans were known dead, dozens more were suspected dead, the bodies of several victims were retrieved to protect them from mutilation and others were probably collected and disposed of by the guilty to protect themselves—and this didn't even include the number of victims accidentally slain by law enforcement personnel. An exact body count was impossible, but bringing the murderers (or as many of the murderers as possible) to justice was an achievable goal and arguably justified inexactitude in terms of the immediately quantifiable dead. The Anderson County Sheriff's Department and the Texas Rangers accepted Gardner's mandate and applied themselves to the process of parsing fact from fiction and tracking down the guilty via paths littered with death.

On August 1, Judge Gardner reconvened his district's already held-over grand jury and instructed it carefully and specifically:

When you were impaneled I called your respectful attention to the oath that you had taken and the special part I called your attention to was as follows: "You shall present no person from envy, hatred or malice, neither shall you leave any person unpresented for love, favor, affection, or hope of reward; but you shall present things truly as they come to your knowledge, according to your understanding, so help you God."

At the time you took that oath none of us dreamed or thought that anything would happen before you were discharged, equal to what has happened. Nobody anticipated any such trouble. And when you were about to be discharged last Saturday, it was supposed that you were about through with your duties, but news coming of this great trouble in the southeastern part of the county has caused me to have you come back especially to investigate that affair and it is a kind of case that this oath especially applies to.

All of you are white men and I presume all of you are Southern men, and it is your duty now to investigate the killing and murder of a large number of negroes, say of at least eight and possibly ten to twelve or more, whom have been killed in the southeastern part of your county by men of your color. Now, if there is any man on this jury that feels he is not equal to the occasion to live up to that oath—why, if it was an original proposition and the jury was just being organized and had not been sworn in, I would suggest to him that he withdraw and asked to be excused so that some other could be put on the jury, but all of you have been sworn in and it would be an embarrassing situation if any man should ask to be excused from the jury; but if there is any man on that jury that cannot live up to that oath he should ask the foreman to excuse him while it is investigating this case.[17]

After these instructions, Judge Gardner went over the statutes regarding threats to take life, conspiracy and principals and accomplices:

I call attention to threats and conspiracies for two reasons. That if any threat had been previously made against any white person or against negroes, investigation should be made and indictments returned, if any. I also want to say that even if there had been such threats or conspiracies on the part of any number of persons or negroes to do violence to white persons, it would not justify anybody to take the law in their own hands. The law furnishes ample remedy and it would be no excuse for shooting down anybody that had made a threat or entered into a conspiracy, but the men should have come up and had them arrested and prosecuted for threats or conspiracy. I do not know that there has been anything of that sort, but in such cases as this, there are always such claims as that, but that is no justification for shooting a man in the back, waylaying or shooting them in their homes.[18]

Finally, Gardner concluded:

In conclusion, I want to emphasize the fact that I regard this affair the most damaging that could happen in the county, that it is a disgrace not only to the county but to the state, and it is up to this jury to do their full duty in the premises.

The grand jury was composed of jury foreman W.H. Nance, a marble yard businessman from Palestine; A.L. Cornwell, a farmer from Cayuga; H.M. Pinzle, a real estate agent in Palestine; B. Wilson, a Denson Springs farmer; Jessie Waddell, a Brushy Creek farmer; J.D. Frederick, a bookkeeper from Palestine; Clarence Quarles, a merchant from Elkhart; W.H. Dick, an insurance broker from Palestine; C. Roe Hall, a real estate agent from Palestine; Gib Day, a Slocum farmer; Albert Dupuy, a farmer from Tennessee Colony; and J.M. Richie, a farmer from Blackfoot.

IV

The world stands appalled at the wholesale murder of innocent colored men and women in your state; and these wicked and merciless murders have undoubtedly brought a very great disgrace upon Texas. I confidently hope that you will show the outside world that your state is not ruled by mob violence and lawlessness; but that Tex[as] has a governor who will see to it that these cold blooded murderers are punished.
—*G. Milford, Washington, D.C. lawyer, in a letter to Texas governor Thomas M. Campbell, August 2, 1910*

On August 2, Texas Ranger Averitt arrested Mac Reed, Alvin Oliver and Tom Thornton, and Captain Rogers apprehended Booze Wise, all in Palestine. At this point, Anderson County law enforcement officials also took five African Americans (Courtney Dancer, Jack Harley, Tom Jones, Will Thomas and Margaret Wilson) into custody for their own protection; they were material witnesses in the grand jury proceedings.

DATE OF ARREST	NAME OF PRISONER	C...
Aug 1st	F. H. Bailey	M...
" "	Morgan Henry	"
" "	Frank Bridges	"
" 2nd	M. C. Reed	"
" "	Alvin Oliver	"
" "	Sam Thornton	"
" "	Budger H. yoe	"
" 4th	H. J. Ash	Carry...
" 5th	Jim Spurgun Jr	M...
" "	Reagan McKenzie	"
" 6th	Coleman Caldwell	whippi...
" 8th	Will Neal	Theft und...
" "	Geo Rose	" "
" 10	Ben Reed	Gambli...
" "	Nat Muler	"
" 13	Zack Hoods	assault to...
" 14	Curtis Spurger	Murd...
" 24	Henry Shipper	"

Texas Rangers, Company C, arrest records for the Slocum area in August 1910. *Courtesy of the Texas State Library and Archives.*

Judge Gardner reopened the saloons and, excepting the appearance of signs and placards warning African Americans to leave Palestine, a modicum of normalcy returned to the city. Willie Foreman (who had been missing since he and Lusk and Alex Holley were attacked) even turned up.

RECAPITULATION OF ARRESTS MADE IN MONTH		
	BY WHOM ARRESTED	WHERE ARRESTED
	Sergt. J. L. Anders	Palestine
	" " " "	"
	Ed Avriett	Slocum
	Hall Avriett	Palestine
	" "	"
	" "	"
	Capt. J. A. Rogers	"
	Hall Avriett	"
	J. L. Anders	"
	" " "	"
	H Avriett & Adams	"
	J. L. Anders	"
	" " "	"
	" " "	"
	" " "	"
	Hall Avriett	"
L Anders & " "	"
	" " " " "	"

On August 4, 1910, former state representative John A. Mobley's position as assistant attorney general was eliminated by the Texas legislature because it deemed the new post unconstitutional. Judge Gardner—who knew or knew of Mobley[19] from Henderson County—immediately sent a letter to Governor Campbell[20] urging him to "employ Mobley to aid the [Anderson County] District Attorney in the prosecution of the cases for the murder of the negroes at Slocum and near there." Governor Campbell did so.

On August 5, Sergeant Anders arrested Reagan McKenzie and S.C. Jenkins, and after four days of testimony and evidentiary hearings, the grand jury recessed until Wednesday, August 10.

On August 12, Walter Ferguson, Josh Bishop and Alvin Oliver were released from the Anderson County jail, and the grand jury recessed until Monday, August 15.

On Sunday, August 14, some of the Rangers and Dr. E.B. Parsons left Palestine about 4:00 a.m. and headed toward the Slocum and Denson Springs communities. The rumor mill immediately cranked up, and early reports suggested the Rangers were headed back down to the area to quell an additional conflict. In reality, the Rangers revisited the area to summon more witnesses for the grand jury proceedings, and Dr. Parsons was brought along to determine if some of the injured African American eyewitnesses (including Lusk Holley and Charlie Wilson) were healthy enough to appear in court.

On August 14, Sergeant Anders[21] arrested Jim Spurger's brother, Curtis, in Palestine.

On August 17, the Anderson County Fourth District Court Grand Jury stepped forward where the July 1, 1909 Smith County Grand Jury had stepped back. After final testimony by massacre survivors Holley and Wilson, it returned indictments containing charges of first-degree murder against seven white men for the killings of five black men. It was a first for East Texas, if not the state of Texas.

Of the first-degree murder charges based on killings "on or about the 29th, 30th and 31st of July, 1910," Jim Spurger was indicted in two cases, Curtis Spurger in three cases, S.C. Jenkins in three cases, Andrew Kirkwood in three cases, B.J. Jenkins in four cases and Isom Garner in four cases; all were remanded to the Anderson County jail. The seventh suspect was not arrested or named, and every suspect except Curtis Spurger and the unnamed culprit was also charged with the killing of Will Burley in Houston County (the grand jury of which was not scheduled to be in session until October). There were no indictments returned for the slayings of John H. Hays or Alex Holley.

In terms of location and era, the indictments were clearly a victory for Judge Gardner, district attorney T.J. Harris, special assistant prosecutor John A. Mobley and the citizens of Anderson County who wanted the perpetrators of the massacre punished. But, though clearly a remarkable regional precedent, the indictments were not overly impressive in terms of simple math.

The acknowledged dead thus far were Sam Baker, Will Burley, Ben Dancer, John H. Hays, Alex Holley, Cleve Larkin and Dick and Jeff Wilson. Will Burley was killed in Houston County, and his death was not addressed in the Anderson County indictments. The slayings of John H. Hays and Alex Holley were also not addressed by the indictments. The twenty-two charges of first-degree murder the grand jury returned, then, were based on the deaths of Cleve Larkin, Sam Baker, Dick and Jeff Wilson and Ben Dancer. That's more than four killers per victim, and Sam Baker was reportedly slain by a single shotgun blast to the chest at point-blank range.

It is surprising that there were no indictments for the attempted murders of Charlie Wilson or Lusk Holley, and Lusk Holley had been present for the murder of his brother Alex. Was he unable to identify any of his or his brother's attackers? And what of the numerous unidentified corpses?

When Sheriff Black said it would be hard to find out how many African Americans had been killed because there were bodies everywhere, it was not a frivolous claim. The buzzards *were* going to find most of them first.

Except they didn't.

No other remains were ever reported or investigated.

CHAPTER 5

EXODUS, EXILE

I

The problem grows more complicated when we talk about racial cleansings. Even when they are acknowledged, people stumble over how to talk about them. What words should we use to describe what we know? To worry about semantics may seem pedantic, but language is how we understand things. It is no coincidence that people used euphemisms such as "disturbing situations" to describe—or perhaps more accurately disguise—what was occurring. And as we now try to uncover what took place, classifying what we see before us is a vital step in restoring our history.

In the few surviving accounts, the expulsions are described by the physical act of what was occurring. In 1908, for example, Ray Stannard Baker, a crusading white journalist who wrote a prescient series of stories on race relations in his book Following the Colour Line, *discussed how whites would terrorize their black neighbors into leaving a community. He called what he saw "Driving Out Negroes." Others have used terms like "banishment," "forced to flee," or "expulsions." The problem with these phrases is that they describe only the act, not the policy.*

—*Elliott Jaspin,* Buried in the Bitter Waters: The Hidden History of Racial Cleansing in America

In July 1996, a Dallas publication known as the *Minority Opportunity News* (now published as the *North Dallas Gazette*) ran an article entitled "Legacy that

Bears the Scars of the Slocum Slaughter" by Allen R. Gray. In the clip, Gray records the recollections of an African American woman named Mable Willis, in her nineties at the time of the interview and age four at the time of the massacre.

Willis's family lived in Palestine in late July 1910, and her parents offered refuge to black folks who had fled on foot through the woods to escape the bloodshed, some of them having run nonstop for miles.

"All I can remember is all these people," Willis said. "Some of them bleeding, tired and scared—[they] came to our house and lived with us for a spell."

In September 1998, the *Cherokee County Informer* republished Gray's piece as "The Remnants of War" but also included an incredible postscript entitled "1910 Slocum Massacre Survivor Found." In the "Survivor Found" piece, the *Informer*

Among the lucky ones, Preston and Annie Pierson and their children hid during the early stages of the Slocum Massacre and were able to escape to Palestine with life and limbs intact. *Courtesy of Felix Green.*

interviewed Mrs. Elvie Ewell, who was almost seven years old when the massacre occurred.

Ewell's father, Preston Pierson, owned 188 acres of land in the Slocum area at the time and worked cotton on it with his brother, John A. Pierson; his uncle Fred Austin; and his cousins, Bennie and Alvorie Austin. Ewell recalled the end of their joint agricultural efforts.

"The first thing I remember is that it was night," Ewell said. "Daddy and Uncle John were sitting at the table. A group of white men came riding though on horses. They told daddy all the black men had better leave Slocum that night or be killed.

"Daddy and all the men got up and went down to the bottom where the cotton was planted," Ewell continued. "They lay down on the ground between the rows and hid. A white man who was our closest neighbor came to the house that night and got all the women and us children and took us to his farm and hid us there."[22]

That night, a white mob killed Alvorie Austin at his home. Another white mob confronted Ewell's uncle John and crushed his left leg with a tree stump. It later had to be amputated.

Preston Pierson eventually collected his wife and kids from the neighbor's farm, loaded up what few possessions they could carry and left the Slocum area, moving the family to Palestine. Later, they relocated farther north to Frankston.[23]

John A. Pierson and his wife, Estella, had only been married eight months when the massacre occurred, and Estella was six months pregnant with twins. They went into hiding after John was attacked, eventually escaping and settling in Oakwood (a community that stretched into both Freestone and Leon Counties). They went on to have ten children, and according to Pierson's grandson Felix Green (a retired marine and current resident of Oceanside, California), John Pierson never spoke of the massacre.[24]

Maxine Session, former *Cherokee County Informer* publisher and now editor of the *Texas Informer*, is familiar with stories like Ewell's and Pierson's.

In 1910, Session's grandparents on her father's side, Holly and Susan Burley (relatives of Will Burley), resided in the Slocum area, near Ioni Creek, with their two sons, three-year-old John and three-month-old Jessie Jr. (Maxine's father). Jim Spurger lived nearby, and when the bloodshed started, the Burleys were located close to ground zero. Fortunately, however, word of what was happening reached Holly and Susan before the white mobs.

It was midday, and folks were in from the fields to take a break and have lunch. Some sat under shade trees, and others stretched out on a covered

Less lucky, John and Estella Pierson eventually escaped to Palestine after the Slocum Massacre, but not before a white mob cost John his left leg. *Courtesy of Felix Green.*

porch. Not long into the interim, someone came up and told them to run. As Maxine relates it—through the words of her kin who lived it—the informant said, "Go, get out, the white people have lost their minds! They're shooting every black person they see."

Holly and Susan and some of their neighbors gathered their children, grabbed their horses and wagons and whatever else they could collect in a matter of seconds and fled immediately. Others did not want to risk getting caught out in the open on horseback or in wagons; they slid into wooden barrels and floated to safety down Ioni Creek.

Session's forbears moved to Cherokee County. Others, like Marsh Holley, escaped to Palestine or farther north in Anderson County. Some fled even farther.

Most of them never returned.

II

Texas has been hurt and harmed by some of her own people. She has been stricken by those of her own household. Just at a time when the eyes of the world were fixed upon her as never before, when her marvelous resources are attracting the attention of homeseekers and investors and drawing them hither in greater numbers than have ever before been known, when men have begun to learn that the lawless Texas which had been handed down by the tongue of ignorance, prejudice and baseless tradition is a thing of the past, there came an outburst of lawlessness, a riot and revel of brutal butchery, an orgy of man-hunting and life-taking which would have disgraced the darkest corner of Dahomey.[25]

—Houston Chronicle, *April 18, 1910*

Warren Pettinos's great-grandfather—a white man—was on the other side of the massacre.

Pettinos's grandmother, Annie Mae Killgo, was born in Newnan, Georgia, in 1895. Her father, Robert Duke Killgo, relocated the family to the Slocum area, near Ioni Lake, in 1901.

Robert Killgo had family in Anderson County and, after the move, worked as a boilermaker, reportedly taking part in the construction of water towers in the nearby communities of Kaufman and Athens.

By all accounts, the Killgo family at large was respected and civic-minded, C.E. Killgo serving as manager of his district's county elections in 1906, and J.T. Killgo[26] serving as a petit juror for the winter term of the district court in 1909. But in late July 1910, Robert Killgo got involved with a bad strain of the Anderson County citizenry. The details were related repeatedly to Pettinos by his grandmother Annie Mae, who was fifteen years old at the time of the Slocum Massacre.

According to Pettinos, his grandmother had a vivid recollection of the incident. She said it all started when a group of white people in the Slocum area grew suspicious of the local African American population. At some point, a small group of white men discovered a black girl walking down by one of the creeks and confronted her, demanding confirmation of their suspicions. The black girl was reportedly unaware or not forthcoming, so the white men forced her down to the creek's edge and dunked her head under water, holding it there in an attempt to jog her memory. After repeated dunks, the black girl supposedly told her white torturers that the black residents of the Slocum area were going to wait until their white neighbors were in a Slocum church and attack them.

Annie Mae told Pettinos that when the night of the alleged attack came, the white men dropped their wives and kids off at church and had them light up the church—like everyone was inside and nothing was askew—and then waited under cover for their black neighbors to appear.

Ioni Creek and the surrounding bottoms looking west off FM Road 2022. *Author's collection.*

According to Annie Mae, when the blacks showed up, the white men—including her father, Robert—ambushed them and killed sixteen to eighteen black folks and then buried them all in a mass, unmarked grave.[27] After the killings, Robert was concerned that he would be implicated in the bloodshed, so he fled back to Georgia to avoid investigation and prosecution. Annie Mae and the rest of Robert's family stayed behind.

Robert reportedly remained in Georgia for a little over five years and then returned to the Slocum area. His reunion with his family was short-lived; he died of jaundice near Palestine on December 8, 1916.

Annie Mae married Richard Bozeman shortly after the Slocum Massacre, but Bozeman passed away on February 6, 1915. Annie Mae later married again, to World War I hero and French Croix de Guerre, Médaille Militaire and American Distinguished Service Cross recipient Turner E. Campe.[28] During battle, Campe was wounded in hand-to-hand combat and later mustard gassed while attempting to cross the Aisne River. His lungs never recovered from the gassing, and he became an alcoholic. Annie Mae found their marriage difficult but endured until Campe died on January 6, 1942. She never remarried.

Annie Mae remained in the Slocum area, living on or near Lake Ioni for the rest of her days.[29] She discussed the Slocum Massacre with Pettinos at least half a dozen times before her passing on April 17, 1968.

———

The stories passed down to Session and Pettinos from their forebears are not uncommon for anyone whose lineage intersected with or was intersected by the Slocum Massacre.

In April 1910, the census for the Slocum area or Precinct Three (which included Denson Springs and Alder Branch) of Anderson County reported 1,504 white citizens and 567 black citizens; African Americans made up approximately 30 percent of the community. In 1920, the census for the Slocum, Denson Springs and Alder Branch areas reported 3,527 white citizens (including Isom Garner,[30] Walter Ferguson[31] and Jeff Wise[32]) and 640 black citizens (including at least two mixed families).

By 1920, the African American population in the Slocum "township" (as the census referred to it)—which in 1910 was considered a place with a "large negro community" and "a good place for a negro to hide out"[33]—had dwindled to just over 15 percent. And what of the Denson Springs area, where many of the blacks in the region had lived and where the bulk of the falsely reported "armed negroes" were preparing to do battle with their white neighbors? The African American population there was reduced to 51 (2 percent), and the Caucasian numbers increased to 2,229 (98 percent).

A census term that began with the Slocum Massacre saw the percentage of African Americans who lived in the southeastern portion of Anderson County reduced by more than half, documenting not the fallout of a race war but a falling in step with what approached a racial expulsion. Only the most isolated, stubborn or alternativeless African Americans remained, and their numbers were probably matched by others who moved into the region unaware.

CHAPTER 6
FEDERAL DISINTEREST

I

The world was startled recently by the report that a massacre of Jews was impending in Russia. America was asked to use its influence with the czar's government for the Jews' protection from wholesale expulsion and slaughter. Before America is able to act upon those representations there comes the news of as bloody and barbarous a persecution of a weak and defenseless race in this "land of the free and home of the brave" as ever took place in darkest Russia. The tale of the wholesale killing of negroes in Palestine, Texas, must cause every American with any pride of country or hope for its future to hang his head in shame.

—*Reverend S.P.W. Drew,* Washington Post, *August 8, 1910*

While Judge Gardner and others were trying to establish the details of the Slocum Massacre and prosecute the guilty parties in Anderson County, a white citizen in Houston County literally took matters into his own hands, utilizing paper and ink.

On August 1, 1910, Volga postmaster John A. Siddon wrote to Cecil A. Lyon, chairman of the Texas Republican State Executive Committee in Sherman:

> *For Humanities sake if you have any influence with the Federal government prevail on the proper authorities to investigate the conditions that prevail in this country as regards the Negro. Some* [illegible] *20 or 30 colored*

Prominent African American religious leader Reverend Simon P.W. Drew was a cogent critic of defending persecuted people overseas while ignoring them in Texas. *Courtesy of the Library of Congress.*

people were murdered at Slocum in Anderson County, Texas for no other cause than the Lord had made them Black; the State of Texas will have a farce of a trial for a show to the world, but no one will ever be punished for these monstrous crimes. Most every plantation that works any considerable number of Negroes carry on a kind of peonage, for instance they will pay a Negro per day, charge him unheard of prices for the necessities of life as for instance 40 cents per gallon for kerosene 10 cts per Bot[tle] for search light matches with a studied effort to keep the Negro in debt. For the merest infraction of plantation rules they are flogged unmercifully and should they try to indict one of these plantation bosses why they would give him a pass to the Happy Hunting grounds. I am not a lawyer, but there should be a law on the statute books of the nation to punish such practices as these when a state will not. There have been a number of Negroes murdered in this county by whites and no arrests have ever been made. In conclusion, I will say I am a white man, am a Republican on National issues although I vote in the Democratic Primaries. If the United States can abolish such practices as these later I will tell you where to find some guilty parties. Will kindly ask you not to make my name public in connection with this as I would fear assassination.

Lyon examined Siddon's letter and forwarded it to the United States attorney general, George W. Wickersham, on August 15:

The enclosed letter is self-explanatory. I am referring it direct to you in order that the case may be investigated. This letter pertains to what you probably saw in the paper, to the recent massacre of from 18 to 25 negroes and as stated by the writer it is probable that any investigation of this in the state courts would be a farce and I suggest that, from his letter, an investigation by the United States authorities would be in order.

Washington, D. C.,
August 13th, 1910.

Pres. William H. Taft,
Beverly, Mass.

Dear Sir;-

The undersigned have been appointed a Committee by the Colored Ministers -- numbering more than 150 -- of the city of Washington to convey to you the enclosed address to the President and the American people relative to the murdering of 20 or more innocent and unarmed colored men near Palestine, Texas recently. It is the hope of the colored Ministers of this city, and of the many thousands whom they represent, as well as the hope of the colored people throughout America, that you may use the powers of your great Office to suppress lynching, murder and other forms of lawlessness in this country. According to the most recent and reliable statistics there are eight times more murders committed in the United States of America each year, than are committed in Great Britain, and six times more than in France, and five times more than of the German Empire. Our Nation is already the laughing stock of civilized peoples throughout the world, and unless something is done to make human life more valuable and law more universally respected, we feel that our beloved country is doomed to destruction at no distant date. We believe that you are as much interested in the suppression of lawlessness and crime in this country as we are, and we feel confident that you will do all in your power to help bring about this much to be desired end.

We beg, sir, to remain

Yours very respectfully,

J. Milton Waldron
J. Anderson Taylor
W. J. Howard,
COMMITTEE.

Open address to President Taft and the American people from the Colored Minister's Union. *Courtesy of the National Archives & Records Administration, College Park, Maryland.*

THE 1910 SLOCUM MASSACRE

When Lyon hadn't heard from Attorney General Wickersham by August 19, he sent another short note requesting that the attorney general confirm receipt of his original correspondence. Whether Wickersham did confirm receipt of Lyon's letter or respond directly or indirectly to Siddon's concerns is unknown. There was, however, an official response from Wickersham to another concerned party.

In early August 1910, a group of over 150 "colored ministers" from Washington, D.C., formed a committee to draft a letter to President William H. Taft in regards to the Slocum Massacre. On August 13, committeemen J. Milton Waldron, J. Anderson Taylor and W.J. Howard sent Taft a letter and an open statement to the American people.

In the letter, the committeemen implored President Taft to use the powers of his "great office to suppress lynching, murder and other forms of lawlessness" and do something to "make human life more valuable and law more universally respected."

In the address to President Taft and the American people, the committee cogently detailed the African American predicament:

> *To God, the Executive head of the Nation, and the American people we make this appeal as descendants of citizens who were, even in bondage, warm friends of the Southern white people; and who, until a half-hundred years ago made history for others, but none for themselves. Since then we have striven against racial antipathy and the stigma of previous condition, and have rapidly improved in literacy, morals and economic status. In the past we put confidence in Statecraft to save us from exploitation at the behest of the strong, but the best we have ever received from it is not enough to deliver us from the troubles of which we now complain. We sought strength through education, but the more we advance along this line, the greater the discrimination. We have bought land, built homes and established Churches, but those states as desire to do so go on disenfranchising us, lynching our men on frivolous charges and unproved allegations, and widening the chasm which race differentiation has made broad enough. When progress does not promise to save a people, that people is near unto desperation. But let us appeal to the best instincts of men as long as reason has a chance or argument a hearing. While the brotherhood of man is a doctrine of our religion we must believe that this world can be made better, and ultimately set right. There is no wrong that cannot be put away by good men determined to do it. We pledge ourselves to this gigantic task, especially in agitating for the enforcement of the law. It is pitiable to note*

Department of Justice,

CARBON COPY FOR THE FILES.

WRH HSR B

152961-3

August 24, 1910.

Mr. J. M. Waldron,

Washington, D. C.

Sir:

The Department is in receipt, by reference from the President, of your letter to him of the 13th instant, transmitting a petition seeking that Federal action be taken to protect the colored people throughout the country from "lynching, murder and other forms of lawlessness".

The protection of life and property is generally a duty devolving upon the state authorities, and except when the deprivation of life and property involves a violation of some right secured by the Constitution or laws of the United States, the Federal Government can take no action.

Your letter and petition deal with the subject of the treatment of colored persons generally and therefore furnish no facts which would warrant this Department in taking any steps to redress the wrongs complained of.

Should there come to your attention any specific case in which a Federal right is violated and you will submit a detailed statement of the facts, the Department will be glad to take such action as the ends of justice require.

Respectfully,

Acting Attorney General.

A succinct Department of Justice response to the August 13 Colored Minister's Union letter and address to President Taft and the American people. *Courtesy of the National Archives & Records Administration, College Park, Maryland.*

that the white man who makes laws for men of other races to live under has not succeeded in ruling according to the laws he has made, nor has he the courage of fairness or courage to punish himself for the greatest crime against the State—the crime of lynching. Within a month approximately a hundred citizens have suffered death or persecution in a community of the State of Texas. They have been lynched, murdered, burned and persecuted, the State apparently powerless to help them. This sad condition of racial strife, ever present like a smoldering volcano ready to emit the lava of race hatred, makes it imperative for us as Colored Ministers, servants of the public and friends of justice, to make this impassioned protest.

Then the committee called on the United States government to 1) work toward a doctrine of fairness regardless of skin color; 2) ensure government by suffrage and protection of the law; 3) abolish lynching, mob rule and race riots; and 4) intervene as necessary in situations such as the Slocum Massacre as the United States had done in circumstances involving the weak or downtrodden in similar scenarios such as the Chinese Boxer Movement or the slaughter of Jews and Armenians in Russia. The statement insisted that the American government "protect its weak at home" with the same commitment it protected innocents abroad.

Taft forwarded the Colored Minister's Union correspondence to the Wickersham Department of Justice. Its official response was curt and dismissive (and addressed to Waldron alone):

The Department is in receipt, by reference from the President, of your letter to him on the 13th instant, transmitting a petition asking Federal action to be taken to protect colored people throughout the country from "lynching, murder and other forms of lawlessness."

The protection of life and property is generally a duty devolving upon the state authorities, and except when the deprivation of life and property involves a violation of some right secured by the Constitution or laws of the United States, the Federal Government can take no action.

Your letter and petition deal with the subject of the treatment of colored persons in general and therefore furnish no facts which would warrant this Department in taking any steps to redress the wrongs complained of.

Should there come to your attention any specific case in which a Federal right is violated and you will submit a detailed statement of the facts, the Department will be glad to take such action as the ends of justice require.

AN ACT OF GENOCIDE IN EAST TEXAS

Interestingly enough, though the Wickersham Department of Justice and President Taft were indifferent to numerous lynchings in Texas and the mass slaughter of African Americans in Anderson County, they found the lynching of a Mexican national in Edwards County quite compelling, and federal officials got involved.

On November 3, 1910, a twenty-year-old Mexican ranch hand named Antonio Rodriquez was accused of killing Mrs. Lem Anderson near Rocksprings and arrested. On November 4, a local mob removed him from the Rocksprings jailhouse and burned him at the stake.

News of the lynching spread, and within a week, Mexicans were rioting in protest, stoning Americans traveling in Mexico and vandalizing the home of the U.S. consul. On November 11, the Mexican government cancelled all bullfights in Mexico to guard against further anti-American outbursts.

Before the issue came to a head, the Mexican Revolution commenced, and Mexico descended into chaos.

CHAPTER 7

PROSECUTION

I

The white men now confined in the Anderson County jail, charged with murdering negroes some days ago, should, and no doubt will, be given a legal trial. It is high time such conduct be stopped.
—Semi-Weekly Courier-Times *(Tyler), August 13, 1910*

On the evening of Sunday, August 21, 1910, Houston County sheriff John C. Lacy and two Texas Rangers transported the six indicted suspects and two recent arrests, Henry Shipper and G.W. Bailey, to Crockett by night train for an examining trial the following morning. Curtis Spurger was also brought along, but not as a suspect in the Houston murder.

District attorney Tom Harris went down that Monday to represent the state, and Judge Ned Morris appeared to counsel the defendants. To a man, the defendants informed Judge Ed Callier that they waived examination and were again remanded to the Anderson County jail without bail.

On August 25, W.H. Nance, the foreman of the grand jury responsible for the Anderson County indictments, sent a letter to Governor Campbell. In the correspondence, he indicated his concern with District Attorney Harris's term expiring and, equally troubling, that special assistant prosecutor Mobley would be called away or otherwise indisposed.

In late August, Sheriff Lacy arrested Tom Franklin near Augusta for shooting two African Americans in previous weeks. Neither of the victims

Copy of Slocum Massacre suspect Henry Shipper's bail request proceedings on November 14, 1910. *Courtesy of the Houston County Courthouse Archives.*

died, and Franklin denied any connection to the attacks. The Augusta justice of the peace set Franklin's bail at $300, and it was promptly secured. The charges against Franklin were never officially linked to the Slocum Massacre, and there is no evidence they were ever pursued.

On September 10, the *Palestine Daily Herald* announced a new city park dedicated to the memory of John H. Reagan.

Two cases involving the Slocum Massacre moved forward, one based on killings in Anderson County and one involving the murder of Will Burley in Houston County.

On November 14, 1910, the defendants in the Houston County case (Jim Spurger, Isom Garner, Andrew Kirkwood, William Henry, B.J. Jenkins and Henry Shipper) were arraigned, and each pleaded "not guilty" to the charge of first-degree murder. The presiding judge denied every defendant except Shipper bail. Shipper's bail was set at $5,000, and his family and friends—J.J. Shipper, E.M. Shipper, T.T.L. Hassell, O.M. Betsill, J.D. McKeen. J. Ploone, O.A. McDaniel, J.T. Gilmore and M.C. Reed[34]—put up their lands and properties as his surety.

On Wednesday, December 12, the defendants in the Anderson County case were arraigned, and Judge Gardner, on his own motion, announced the trial venue would be changed to Limestone County unless the attorneys for both the state and the defendants agreed to a different location in the counties of Navarro, McLennan, Williamson, Travis or Harris.

Judge Gardner preferred Navarro County, but he also liked Freestone County because the court met there the first Monday in January. The attorneys for the state and the defendants got together and decided on a venue in Harris County.

As the year wound down, the December 23 edition of the *Palestine Daily Herald* ran a conspicuous feature entitled "Fewer Persons Slain by Mobs This Year," perhaps hoping to alleviate local feelings of guilt or reinterpret the last half of the year altogether. It was a national tabulation, and it listed only six lynchings in Texas for the annum, four black (presumably Allen Brooks, Frank Bates, Leonard Johnson and the transient who allegedly attacked Mrs. Hub Bailey) and two white (perhaps one being Antonio Rodriguez). It did not include the Slocum Massacre:

THE CRISIS

RECORD OF THE DARKER RACES

Volume One   NOVEMBER, 1910   Number One

Edited by W. E. BURGHARDT DU BOIS, with the co-operation of Oswald Garrison Villard,
J. Max Barber, Charles Edward Russell, Kelly Miller, W. S. Braithwaite and M. D. Maclean.

CONTENTS

PUBLISHED MONTHLY BY THE

National Association for the Advancement of Colored People

AT TWENTY VESEY STREET   NEW YORK CITY

ONE DOLLAR A YEAR   TEN CENTS A COPY

In November 1910, the first issue of the NAACP's magazine *The Crisis* appeared. Edited by W.E.B. Du Bois, the inaugural edition featured an article that discussed the 1906 "race riot" in Brownsville, Texas, another incident where innocent African Americans were blatantly wronged. *Courtesy of the Library of Congress, General Collections.*

In the foregoing record the word "lynching" has been held to apply only to the summary punishment inflicted by a mob or by any number of citizens on a person alleged to have committed a crime for which that person should have been tried according to the law. This limitation excludes a number of cases reported during the year, such as the race trouble which occurred near Slocum, Texas, last August, in which eight or ten negroes were killed.

The feature also failed to note at least two other lynchings of African Americans reported in Texas in 1910, both of which involved unidentified victims.[35]

II

Ollie Burley lived on Jim Spurger's place, but I was not present when they went down there and talked to him that morning. I suppose we could have gone down there and killed him just as easy as the others.[36] That insolent manner and conduct of the negroes commenced at the time that negro was burned in Cherokee county for raping and murdering that white child; it seemed to me it did. The negroes down there are not disbehaving now.[37]
—An excerpt from Alvin Oliver's testimony that was introduced at the habeas corpus appeal hearing of Jim Spurger et al on May 10, 1911, at the state court of criminal appeals

Initially, Judge Gardner's efforts to bring some of the folks responsible for the Slocum Massacre to justice were coordinated and effective, aided by Governor Campbell in the person of special assistant prosecutor Mobley, Sheriff Black and a determined lead prosecutor in district attorney T.J. Harris. But elections have consequences.

The new district attorney, Earl Adams Jr., was the son of Earl Adams Sr., one-third of the Judge Ned Morris–led *Spurger et al* defense team. Sheriff Black was replaced by Lee Boyd. And when the new governor, Oscar Branch Colquitt, took over on January 17, 1911, he didn't keep special assistant prosecutor Mobley involved or make sure Harris stayed on as special assistant prosecutor to ensure prosecutorial continuity.

On April 25, 1911, the Houston County case, like its Anderson County counterpart, did receive a change of venue:

The Court being satisfied that a trial alike fair and impartial to the accused and the state cannot be had in this Houston County on account of the motion of the cause, and the circumstances attending the investigation and the great excitement growing out of the killing of so many negroes together with the large number of defendants indicted and otherwise implicated and the vigorous actions of the officers in bringing about an investigation and the commendation of such action by a great number of people and consideration by others—has caused many to form and express opinions as to the merits of the case and as to what should be done, and the frequent mingling of people from the immediate neighborhood of the trouble at Crockett, with the people from all parts of the county, disqualifying jurors in the county to such extent as to render it improbable that a jury alike fair and impartial to the state and the defendants could be procured. [38]

The Houston County case was also moved to Harris County, and Andrew Kirkwood was granted bail at $1,500.

On Wednesday, May 3, 1911, defense counsel Judge Ned Morris filed a writ of habeas corpus in the state court of criminal appeals regarding Case 7325, attempting to secure bail for Jim Spurger, B.J. Jenkins, S.C. Jenkins, Curtis Spurger and Isom Garner.

On Wednesday, May 10, the court of criminal appeals reversed Judge Gardner's denial of bail to the remaining incarcerated defendants, and soon most of them posted $1,500 sureties and were released.

Judge Gardner summed up the rest in his *Memoirs*:

In those days the prosecuting attorney's principal pay came from fees for convictions, and the district or county attorney for Harris County felt that he could not put his time in on prosecuting white men for killing negroes in another county.

The Slocum Massacre cases languished in Harris County and were never prosecuted.

———

In 1916, Judge Gardner encountered Spurger while campaigning in Elkhart. Gardner tried to avoid him, explaining the situation to a friend, Dr. Joseph

CASE NO	DEFENDANT SURNAME	DEFENDANT GIVEN NAME	OFFENSE	DISPOSITION OF CASE	MO	DY	YEAR	DOCK NO	PAGE
3958 1/2	Soloman	Sam	Perjury	Discharged	5	31	1895	1	509
5744	Spurlock	Walter	Unlaw. sell-ing liquor	Dismissed	11	15	1919	D-12 6	161 255
7031	Spence	Will	Burglary	2 years in Pen	10	22	1906	3 2	474 576
7031	Spence	Will	Burglary	Acquitted	11	19	1906	4 5	45 225
7270	Spurlock	Jonn	Theft of hogs	Dismissed	3	28	1910	6	14 24
7325	Spurger et al	Jim	Murder	Plea of not guilty	10	14	1910	6 6	33 40
7325	Spurger et al	Jim	Murder	Transf to Harris Co	4	25	1911	6 6	41 59
7327	Spurger	Jim	Assault to murder	Dismissed	4	19	1913	6 6	33 104
7744	Spurlock	Walter	V-L-O-L	Indicted	11	24	1914	4	191
7805	Spencer	Joe	Theft of hogs	Dismissed	4	27	1917	6 D-12	184 91
8638	Spillers	Darias	Theft of cattle	Dismissed	11	10	1926	6 6	368 371
9597	Sparks	Herbert	False imprisonment	Transf to County Co	11	8	1937	8 8	58 50

Reproduced page from the index of the *Houston County Court Criminal Minutes*. There is no mention of a separate case against Jim Spurger in most of the local newspapers of the time, but he was charged with assault to commit murder (Case 7327) in addition to the original Slocum Massacre–related murder offense (Case 7325). Spurger initially claimed he was attacked by an African American on the outset of the hostilities and killed his attacker in self-defense. His attacker/victim was never identified, and this claim was never substantiated. *Courtesy of the Houston County Courthouse Archives.*

Harper Paxton. Paxton thought Gardner might be being overcautious and advised him to shake Spurger's hand and treat him like any other voter.

When Judge Gardner extended his hand, Spurger grabbed it and struck him in the face with his free hand. Judge Gardner grabbed Spurger's collar, but several men stepped in and broke up the incident before it went any further.

Dr. Paxton attended to Gardner's minor wounds, and another friend, Will Weatherford, supplied Gardner with a handgun to protect himself for the remainder of his stay. Judge Gardner then bought his own pistol and began carrying it with him for out-of-town campaign events.

Later, Judge Gardner[39] ran into another Slocum Massacre suspect:

> *I got out of my buggy in Eustace* [Henderson County] *and a man ran into me like he was crazy. I said, "Who are you?" and he said "Kirkwood." I grabbed him in his collar and put my pistol in his belly and said "I'll shoot the life out of you." He jerked loose and ran to a constable and his*

deputy saying that I had a pistol. The officers came up, took hold of me and demanded the pistol, and we went into the office of the Justice of the Peace. I asked for the statutes and after reading the pistol law, I explained that I was a traveler and had been attacked by one of the murderers of the Slocum negroes and had been advised by the sheriffs of Houston and Anderson Counties to carry a pistol, and said, "If you are not satisfied, call up Judge Prince." The Justice of the Peace said he was satisfied I had a right to carry the pistol and handed it back to me. Later, at home, I walked out to the lot with my son Howard to try our hand at shooting the pistol. I then learned about the safety feature and realized that if it had been necessary for me to shoot when Kirkwood, one of the Slocum murderers ran into me I would not have known how to do it.

CHAPTER 8

CATACLYSMS

I

Why make a new Constitution, why pay for sessions of the Legislature, or maintain courts and judges if men are to thus take life when they will and go their way unwhipped of justice? It really appears to be farcical in the extreme to have all the machinery running, three departments of government in operation and a constitutional convention in full blast, scores of men arguing with great eloquence as to what the law shall be, when the law is thus walked over openly and defiantly by bands and gangs of influential and respectable outlaws.

—Dallas Morning News, *July 12, 1901*

At one or two o'clock in the morning on January 6, 1913, the Anderson County Courthouse was destroyed by what the *Palestine Daily Visitor* described as an "immense conflagration." By the time the Palestine Fire Department was on the scene, the fire was well established on the second floor, and the water pressure at the two available hydrants was too insufficient to have much effect on the raging flames. The firefighting effort quickly became a salvage operation.

Firefighters joined awakened citizens in a courageous attempt to save as much of the courthouse's holdings as possible; they ran in and out with furnishings, books and documents. The district courtroom and the entire criminal court docket were incinerated. The county surveyor's office

Left and opposite: View of the Anderson County Courthouse before (circa 1900) and after two men attempted to burn down the building in order to eliminate evidence against one on January 6, 1913. *Courtesy of the Anderson County Historical Commission.*

was destroyed. The offices of the county judge, treasurer and clerk were spared but damaged by what water the fire department was able to apply to the blaze. The offices of the tax assessor and the tax collector were broken into, and salvagers tossed the books out the window to assistants below, who in turn transported them to the Old Town Drugstore for temporary storage.

The firefighters and citizens who responded to the fire remained on the scene until 9:00 a.m. the following day. The criminal docket was suspended for two weeks, and all lost indictments had to be rewritten.[40]

Though many of the papers and possessions of the county officials themselves were not insured, the courthouse itself was. It was rebuilt in 1914.

It was later discovered that two arsonists were responsible for the fire in an attempt to destroy incriminating evidence against one of them. The ploy was unsuccessful because most of the actual court records were housed in fireproof vaults.

If you call down to the Anderson County property records office today, they are likely to tell you that most of the documents concerning properties in 1910 were destroyed in the fire or lost. When descendants of the victims of the Slocum Massacre are able to track down any pertinent property record paperwork, they often claim it has been altered to make the loss or transfer of their ancestors' lands and property look aboveboard.

Some of the black families who fled the area after the massacre carried the deeds to their land with them and typically sold them quickly and cheaply afterward. Others fled with little more than the clothes on their backs and were entirely dispossessed, their former white neighbors free to take or repurpose African American property and possessions as they saw fit.

Scenes of Anderson County Court House Following the Big Fire

Scene at Early Morning

View Taken Later in Day

The above views show the appearance of Anderson county's court house, following the fire Monday morning, which practically destroyed it called to the second photograph, showing the appearance of the wall lines after the roof had fallen. The building makes a better appearance

II

Fanatics in power and the funnel of a tornado have this in common—the narrow path in which they move is marked by violence and destruction.

—Oscar Ostlund

On Wednesday, April 24, 1929, a massive tornado tore through Slocum, killing seven and wounding approximately two dozen.

THE 1910 SLOCUM MASSACRE

An area one mile wide and ten miles long was strewn with structural wreckage, uprooted trees and dead livestock, evidencing the path of the cyclonic devastation. Every residential and commercial building was damaged or demolished. Bolts of cloth from a local general store had flown up into trees and unfurled, revealing massive, surreal ribbons that swayed in the wind. A mule, still alive, was found in a tree. A wagon with a team of horses still hitched was carried away and strewn dead in a nearby pasture. Another horse with a two-by-four sticking out of its back survived.

The seven human casualties included Mr. and Mrs. P.E. McDaniel, Mrs. Ben Kirkwood and her two sons (ages four and seven), Edna Gatlin and nine-year-old Claude McIver. The list of injured included Bud Gatlin and his son, Harry; Elvie Dunham; Henry, Ben, Maudie and Carl Kirkwood; J.C. and I.E. McIver; ten-year-old Nellie Tucker; one-year-old Nolan Dickey; Eunice Miller; Emma Betsill;[41] Jack, James and J.W. Vickery; Charles E. Turner; Lloyd Taylor; Wynne McDaniel; and Raymond Raines.

The surrounding communities (especially Palestine and Grapeland) came to Slocum's aid immediately, sending Red Cross volunteers to assist the wounded and homeless and collecting food, clothing and supplies for the victims of the storm. They also organized local members of the American Legion and the Boy Scouts to patrol the district and discourage looters.

On May 14, 1929, toddler Nolan Dickey became the eighth victim of the tornado, succumbing to cranial injuries he suffered during the storm.

On June 21, the Texas legislature approved $15,000 in disaster aid for Slocum Consolidated School District No. 5 of Anderson County, allotting $13,500 for replacing the school building and facilities at Slocum and $1,500 for the construction of a one-room primary school building at Phillips Springs.

If the rapid response and rebuilding of Slocum had all the early makings of a success story, it should have because it was. But the coordinated regional response and swift, effective governmental interest and action this natural cataclysm inspired clearly highlighted the lack thereof during and after the unnatural cataclysm of 1910. And in retrospect, the two are inextricably linked.

In the case of the 1929 tornado, all of the reported injured and dead were white, and most of the families involved were residents of the Slocum area in the 1910 census. No African American casualties or injuries were mentioned. This either profoundly demonstrates the successful nature of the Slocum

Massacre as genocide or expulsion or suggests that race relations after the 1910 massacre had declined so profoundly that the possible tornado-related injuries or deaths of African Americans in the community went unrecorded because they were of little interest or the black community had become completely isolated. If the former was the case, superstitious folks in and outside the area—and particularly some of the refugees of the massacre—suspected this cataclysm was divine intervention or karmic retribution. It is unclear if the three Kirkwoods who perished and four who were injured were related to Andrew Kirkwood, but the matching surname certainly lent credence to suspicions of the superstitious.

CHAPTER 9

1984

I

The past was erased, the erasure was forgotten, the lie became truth.
—George Orwell, 1984

In the preface to Armistead Albert Aldrich's *The History of Houston County, Texas* (1943), Aldrich devotes a section to a horrible incident. "No history of Houston County would be complete," he writes, "without an account of the terrible massacre that occurred there in October 1838, known as the Edens-Madden Massacre, which occurred at the home of John Edens, on San Pedro Creek, about 12 or 13 miles North East of Crockett."

At the time, a significant number of the local male citizenry had accompanied San Jacinto hero Captain William Turner Sadler[42] on the Cordova-Kickapoo Expedition with Major Leonard Mabbit. A few families in the area had relocated to the home of John Edens, where he and James Madden, Martin Murchison and Elias Moore were on hand to protect families while many of the men folk were away. The Edens residence consisted of two cabins separated by a covered breezeway. The women and children—Lucinda Edens and her daughters, Emily, Caledonia and Melissa; Mrs. John Madden and her three sons, Balis, Robert and Seldon; Nancy Halhouser Madden and her daughter Mary; and Mrs. John Murchison and her stepdaughter-in-law, Mary Murchison Sadler (wife of William Turner Sadler)—were assigned to one cabin, and the four men (listed above) took

A Texas historical marker (located in Hayes Park in Augusta) commemorating the 1838 Edens-Madden Massacre. The quasi-identified "Negro" woman in the last line of the text was the only "Anglo" hero of the incident. *Author's collection.*

the other. An African American (presumably a slave) named Patsy or Betsy occupied a small servant's quarters in the yard.

On or about the evening of October 19, the occupants of the Edens residence turned in, and one cabin was subsequently attacked by a band of Indians. They broke down the door to the room occupied by the women and children, killing Mrs. Murchison and Mary Sadler[43] immediately. Mrs. Edens sustained vicious knife and tomahawk wounds but fled across two fence lines and died in a nearby field. Balis Madden escaped during the commotion and slid into a hog pen, later hiding among local slaves.[44]

The room itself caught fire, and Mrs. Robert Madden, also seriously wounded, struggled across the breezeway and entered the men's room, collapsing on one of the beds. The startled men fled.

When the attack began, Patsy (or Betsy) grabbed Melissa Edens and fled a mile and a half to the Davis residence, delivering her to safety. Then she returned to the Edens home and rescued Mrs. James Madden from the bed in the men's room before the roof collapsed, carrying Mrs. Madden to the servant's quarters and placing her in her own bed. Patsy (or Betsy) then hurried back into the collapsing structures and spotted Nancy Madden, who had sustained three serious tomahawk wounds. Patsy (or Betsy) rescued Nancy Madden as well and transported her to the servant's quarters, where she cared for them both until help (and the men away on the Cordova-Kickapoo Expedition) returned the next day.

Excepting Melissa Edens and Balis Madden, the children perished at the hands of the Indians or in the flames or were carried into captivity. Eight women and children died or were unaccounted for. The Madden wives survived and were still living in the Augusta area almost half a century later.

This anecdote is important for two reasons.

First, the obvious hero of the Edens-Madden Massacre was a black woman, probably a slave. She ran in while four white men ran away. She rescued one woman the white men assumed was dead and another woman the men didn't even bother to look for. And the local white recorders of history weren't even able to verify her name. Even the historical marker that commemorates the event identifies her as "Patsy or Betsy, a Negro woman."

Second, Aldrich insisted that "no history of Houston County would be complete" without a telling of the Edens-Madden Massacre but glaringly omitted the Slocum Massacre, of which he—in turn, as local lawyer, judge, legislator and historian in the area for decades—was well aware. In fact, many of the citizens in northeast Houston County referred to it as the Slocum-Augusta Massacre, and more Houston County residents probably perished in it than in the Edens-Madden Massacre. And some of those residents might have been descendants of Patsy or Betsy, the "Negro" heroine.

The year after Aldrich's *The History of Houston County, Texas* was published, Lusk Holley was shot and killed in Oakwood. World War II was raging, and a group of white Oakwood locals gave a young, mentally challenged man a gun and told him to keep an eye out for Japanese soldiers. They then identified Lusk as a Japanese soldier.

On February 24, 1944, the mentally challenged man subsequently shot Lusk in the neck and chest, and Lusk died shortly thereafter.[45] The pranksters were never charged, and the mentally challenged "patriot" was reportedly tried and found not guilty by reason of insanity.

II

I did not fully understand all of what was happening, but I recognized fear in the faces of the black people who came to see my father that night. I heard the terror in their excited but hushed voices as they told him what was happening. The image that stands out most clearly in my mind is of bare, black feet, scratched and cut, below trousers and skirts that were torn and soiled from their fourteen-mile flight across fields and through woods to seek papa's help.
　—*Jerry Sadler,* Politics, Fat-Cats & Honey-Money Boys *(1984)*

Forty-one years after Aldrich tried to consign the Slocum Massacre to oblivion, the efforts of two other prominent Houston County natives reintroduced it. The first was Jerry Sadler, great-grandson of W.T. Sadler and Texas politician and folk hero, once described by the *Austin American-Statesman* as the "fighting champ of Texas politics."

In a 1938 race for a seat on the Texas Railroad Commission, Sadler was reportedly involved in fifty-eight fistfights and won the election if not all the physical confrontations. In later stints as a state representative and Texas railroad commissioner, he was old school and intimidating. He resisted desegregation, fought to keep spittoons in the state capitol, criticized sideburns and miniskirts and punched and poked fellow state representatives if he felt the situation or his honor required it. In 1969, after a scandal involving recovered treasure from Spanish galleons (sunk by a hurricane in 1553) discovered in Texas tidelands off the coast of Padre Island, he became the first politician in Texas history to be censured. But before fame, power and infamy, he was a toddler growing up near Grapeland, and one of his first memories was defined by the Slocum Massacre.

Not quite three years old, Sadler—like Mable Willis, twenty-three miles farther north—witnessed the shock, terror and bewilderment on the faces of the refugees of the Slocum Massacre. He saw the torn clothes and the bloody feet and ankles they sustained in their trek to his father's (Claude Sadler) place. And what he didn't comprehend at the time, his father, brothers or an African American named "Deaf and Dumb Gus" Barnett explained to him as he got older.

A medium-sized group of African Americans, mostly composed of the Barnett family—which included Gus Barnett—showed up at the Sadler doorstep on the evening of Saturday, July 30. They were exhausted and bloody from their flight, and they claimed that a white mob of approximately forty men was shooting down any black folks they came upon. The Barnett group was also concerned the mob was on its trail.

Claude Sadler instructed his eldest son, Robert, to make sure the Barnett clan was fed and given clean clothes and, all except for Gus, relocated to the hayloft of his barn. Though deaf and dumb, Gus was known as the best shot in Anderson County, even in Caucasian circles. Claude and his friend Bob Scarborough took Gus with them into Grapeland to get guns and ammunition. They got back to the Sadler place less than an hour before the white mob appeared. Claude sent Gus to the Sadler smokehouse with a double-barreled shotgun (and plenty of ammunition) and stationed the rest of the Barnett men at the farmhouse with guns.

When the white mob arrived, Claude and Bob were sitting in the horse buggy they

Jerry Sadler was a Democratic politician in Texas. As a child, he witnessed some of the effects of the Slocum Massacre and later said the experience compelled him toward a life of public service. *Courtesy of Anderson County Historical Commission, Palestine, Texas.*

had taken to town, and Claude was short on salutations. He simply informed the marauders that a number of armed Negroes had them in their sights from the farmhouse and "Deaf and Dumb Gus" had a double barrel trained on them from the smokehouse. Claude advised them to turn around and go home, and that's what they did.

"Deaf and Dumb Gus" would recount the story to Jerry several times over the years, using his own form of sign language, extending two fists in unison four times to indicate the forty-member white mob and two extended fingers to represent Claude Sadler and Bob Scarborough. According to Jerry's family and Gus, the mob's impasse at the Sadler place was the end of the carnage, and when the massacre would later come up in conversation, the African Americans in the area referred to it as "Bad Saturday" rather than as the Slocum or Slocum-Augusta Massacre. They also had some names to add to the official list of the dead. The Barnett clan lost two of its own, and Jerry's family and Gus claimed Ned Larkin was killed, along with a young woman named Rae and her infant child.

No names of members of the mob were passed down to Jerry, but his father and brothers would later describe them as "white men from prominent and powerful families." And Jerry and his family felt the whole affair had been a land grab from the beginning. "The truth is simply that the whites wanted the land that the blacks owned," he said, "and they had decided finally that there was only one way to get it."

Jerry Sadler passed away on February 26, 1982. His memoir, *Politics, Fat-Cats & Honey-Money Boys*, was published posthumously in 1984.

III

I was born in 1910 and every negro was killed from Slocum to the road known as 227.

—*Dr. Granville James Hayes, MD*

On February 28, 1984, almost exactly two years from the day of Sadler's death, Houston County Historical Commission chairwoman Eliza H. Bishop sent a letter to Dr. Granville James Hayes of Alvin, Texas. Dr. Hayes was born in Augusta on November 10, 1910, less than four months after the Slocum Massacre. His father, J.W. Hayes, was a prominent doctor in the area.

A Texas historical marker commemorating the exceptional doctors of the Augusta community, including J.W. Hayes, who sheltered his family's black nanny during the Slocum Massacre and witnessed the aftermath. *Author's collection.*

Dr. Granville Hayes had donated a small parcel of land (assumed to be a quarter acre) to Houston County for a group of four historical markers in Augusta in 1970. He no longer lived in the area but still had the land. One of the markers commemorated the aforementioned Edens-Madden

Massacre, and another was devoted to outstanding early physicians of Augusta, including Dr. Hayes's father.

With sesquicentennial celebrations ahead for Texas (1986) and Houston County (1987), Bishop wrote to Dr. Hayes in an attempt to procure an extension of the original quarter-acre parcel that Dr. James had donated to include a structure the county might utilize for sanitary facilities. On March 2, Dr. Hayes wrote back indicating that he would agree to donate the rest of the land but had one stipulation:

> *There will be one restriction placed on the gift. I know you know there is a plaque about the Indian Massacre in which 3 people were killed. What you don't have that I am sure many of the white people are very much ashamed of is that a greater massacre occurred which you do not mention.*

Dr. Hayes went on to relate that his family had been in the middle of the Houston County side of the Slocum Massacre:

> *I had a letter that mother wrote to my half sister Jimmie telling her of the horrors of the negro rising. The streets of Priscilla [Percilla] were barricaded and the men patrolled the barricades for at least 2 nights thinking that there was an army of blacks coming. The actual truth is there never was a negro uprising. There were 2 half renters, one was a half renter on my father's place, that started the rumor. One was named Jim Spurger and the other was named Andrews.[46] An article on this can be found in the archives of a paper in Palestine that was being published at that time. The reason I know this is many years ago I did a survey and found it was still there and I have since lost it. The survey said there were 18 people killed and for the first time in the history of Texas a white man went to the penitentiary for killing a black man. Jim Spurger and this Andrews, whose first name I have forgotten, both were indicted and convicted and spent 2 and ½ years in the penitentiary.[47] I cannot give the name but one of the best friends I ever had that I grew up with, his father rode with the vigilantes. He was a fine and religious man and when he found out that it had been a false alarm he committed suicide. I grew up with all of that and I have heard these things told by my father many times.*

When Dr. Hayes was a young man, two men involved in the massacre told him that they had dug a common grave for their victims in the playground area of the Silver Creek School.[48] They admitted to placing eight or nine dead African Americans into it and then covering them up, tamping the loose dirt so the bare ground there looked no different than it did any other time the kids played on it.

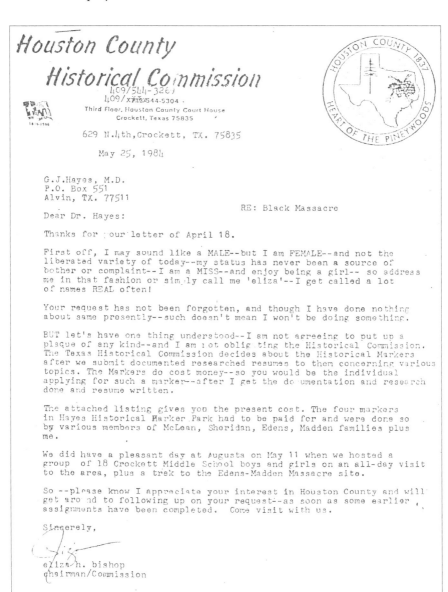

Houston County Historical Commission

409/544-326)
409/x713544-5304.
Third Floor, Houston County Court House
Crockett, Texas 75835

629 N.4th, Crockett, TX. 75835

May 25, 1984

G.J.Hayes, M.D.
P.O. Box 551
Alvin, TX. 77511

RE: Black Massacre

Dear Dr. Hayes:

Thanks for your letter of April 18.

First off, I may sound like a MALE--but I am FEMALE--and not the liberated variety of today--my status has never been a source of bother or complaint--I am a MISS--and enjoy being a girl-- so address me in that fashion or simply call me 'eliza'--I get called a lot of names REAL often!

Your request has not been forgotten, and though I have done nothing about same presently--such doesn't mean I won't be doing something.

BUT let's have one thing understood--I am not agreeing to put up a plaque of any kind--and I am not obligating the Historical Commission. The Texas Historical Commission decides about the Historical Markers after we submit documented researched resumes to them concerning various topics. The Markers do cost money--so you would be the individual applying for such a marker--after I get the documentation and research done and resume written.

The attached listing gives you the present cost. The four markers in Hayes Historical Marker Park had to be paid for and were done so by various members of McLean, Sheridan, Edens, Madden families plus me.

We did have a pleasant day at Augusta on May 11 when we hosted a group of 18 Crockett Middle School boys and girls on an all-day visit to the area, plus a trek to the Edens-Madden Massacre site.

So --please know I appreciate your interest in Houston County and will get around to following up on your request--as soon as some earlier assignments have been completed. Come visit with us.

Sincerely,

eliza h. bishop
chairman/Commission

May 25, 1984 letter from Eliza H. Bishop, chairwoman of the Houston County Historical Commission, to Dr. Granville J. Hayes. Dr. Hayes was lobbying for a historical marker dedicated to the Slocum Massacre. *Courtesy of Houston County Historical Commission.*

A different individual involved in the massacre shared another gruesome anecdote. He told Dr. Hayes he was with a group that rode up on an African American's house and began firing into it with their guns. He said that a black child approximately six years old jumped out the back door and ran toward a fenced peach orchard. He claimed that Jim Spurger jumped the orchard fence on horseback and began firing at the boy, missing him four times. Spurger's fifth shot struck the fleeing child between the shoulders and "blew his heart right out through his chest anteriorly."

Dr. Hayes also touched on what was probably the Jerry Sadler narrative, indicating that he had heard the white bloodshed ended when one of Spurger's raids was repelled by a black man with a shotgun (presumably "Deaf and Dumb Gus").

Dr. Hayes relayed the details of the incident to Bishop as well as he could and indicated he wanted "the factual story of the massacre of the negros from Slocum to Augusta" researched and commemorated with a historical marker.

On March 31, Bishop responded, reporting that the Houston County Historical Commission members had agreed to research the massacre of African Americans after prior commitments had been fulfilled. Bishop also indicated that their workload was heavy, and she wouldn't commit to a timeline.

On April 18, Dr. Hayes answered Bishop's letter with further details, mostly minor, and a reiteration. "As I told you I will reconsider and probably give you the balance of the land including the building," he wrote, "after this has been researched to my satisfaction and you have agreed to put up a plaque at the park labeled 'The Massacre of Blacks by the Whites as Reported in this Palestine Paper,'" if you can find it.

On May 25, Bishop responded, assuring Dr. Hayes that his request had not been forgotten but also clarifying her position:

> *BUT let's have one thing understood—I am not agreeing to put up a plaque of any kind—and I am not obligating the Historical Commission. The Texas Historical Commission decides about the Historical Markers after we submit documented researched resumes to them concerning various topics.*

Bishop then assured Dr. Hayes that the commission would address his request when time permitted, attached a historical marker pricelist and invited him to attend a commission meeting.

On October 12, Dr. Hayes, presumably frustrated, attempted to circumvent Bishop and wrote directly to J.L. Beaird, the district engineer of the Crockett region's Texas Highway Department. He was seventy-four years old at the time and was concerned that the number of people who still remembered the bloodshed was rapidly dwindling. He shared the basic background of the massacre and briefly detailed the historical marker process he was involved in with Bishop. Things were not going as well as he would have liked, and he didn't feel Bishop was receptive to a marker dedicated to the massacre:

> *The only thing that I am anxious to be placed there is a marker of the negro massacre that occurred in 1910. All black people were killed that could be caught from Slocum to road 227 as it is called now, from Grapeland to Augusta. My father was practicing medicine at this time at Priscilla [Percilla] which is only 3 miles from the road from Grapeland to Augusta, the one we are talking about known as 227 now. I wrote to a paper in Palestine in the 1930s and they went back in the files and found a report of this massacre of the black people. In this report it said only 18 were killed. My father and other of my relatives who were living there from the time I was old enough to remember told me the actual fact was that there was never any official count but my father was sure he knew of at least 20 to 30 who were killed in their efforts to get away from the white vigilante committee. I can remember that going from Priscilla [Percilla] on the old road back to 227 that there must have been 30 or 40 negro shacks where black people had lived before but which all of them were killed or driven away during this vigilante committee which was led by a half renter on my father's place named Jim Spurger and another man whose name was Andrews. The black people never returned and now there are no black people in that area.*[49]

On October 26, Beaird replied to Dr. Hayes, noting that he was forwarding a copy of their correspondence to Bishop and suggesting that Dr. Hayes submit his recommendations for recognition to the Houston County Historical Commission.

When Bishop received Beaird's letter, she forwarded it and copies of all of her correspondence with Dr. Hayes to Dan Utley, director of the Texas Historical Commission's Research and Markers Department. Bishop indicated that she felt obligated to keep Utley abreast of the situation, as Dr. Hayes had contacted the state Department of Highways directly, but she also made light of the affair, beginning her letter, "Methinks Hallowe'en is appropriate for the THC, you and Frances to become aware of the individual and project named herein."

Bishop noted that no research regarding Dr. Hayes's "black massacre" had been performed on her part because she was still preoccupied with

There were exceptions to the racist elements in the region where the Slocum Massacre occurred. One was the Mary Allen Seminary in Crockett. Founded in 1886, it was the first school in Texas devoted solely to educating black women and, in 1924, became the first black women's college. It was open until 1972. *Author's collection.*

other issues. Then Bishop reported an interesting turn in the Houston County Historical Commission's pursuit of additional land from Dr. Hayes. "Regarding the quarter of an acre," she said, "since we are now a recognized part of Houston County, we have discovered that the quarter of an acre did not exist."

On October 29, Bishop also wrote to the chairman of the Anderson County Historical Commission, Oliver B. McReynolds, requesting help in finding information on Dr. Hayes's "black massacre." Whether McReynolds ever formally responded is unknown. But a cursory examination of the Houston County property records yielded a bill of sale transferring Dr. Hayes's quarter acre to the Houston County Historical Survey Committee on May 20, 1970—except it was never a quarter acre. It was 0.467 acre of land, closer to a half acre, which meant the quarter acre Bishop was pursuing had been procured with the original quarter acre in 1970.

In retrospect, it's curious that Bishop concluded that the additional quarter acre did not exist when it or a parcel approaching a quarter acre obviously did. There is no evidence that the Houston County Historical Commission ever improved any portion of the expanded parcel, but perhaps Bishop was simply being prudent. As the Houston County Historical Commission's prior projects stretched out and Dr. Hayes's request was slow to be addressed, he began giving interviews concerning the Slocum Massacre, and his comments regarding the commission's attention to the issue were probably less than flattering. In her letter to McReynolds, Bishop regards Dr. Hayes's interviews as "quite a bit of unwise publicity for the incident as well as unsavory."

At some point, all we are left with regarding Dr. Hayes's one-man historical marker effort is conjecture. Was he running a bluff to get the Slocum Massacre marker erected, knowing all along that the Houston County Historical Survey already owned the desired land? Perhaps.

Did Bishop deny that the previously coveted additional approximate quarter acre existed just to defuse the subject and squelch talk of it at a time when the wildly important sesquicentennial celebrations were just around the corner? Possibly.

But there were additional motives.

In 1979, the Houston County Historical Commission assembled and published the *History of Houston County, Texas, 1687–1979*, but it was no secret that Bishop was its author. Like Aldrich, Bishop's *History* makes no mention of the Slocum Massacre, the Slocum-Augusta Massacre or Bad Saturday. It was a major event to leave out of a county history, embarrassing if done so unaware and shameful if purposefully ignored.

And then there was the reputation of Houston County itself. Bishop might have seen no point in dredging up this egregious incident and seeing her home county besmirched. [50]

At the time of her death in 2009, Bishop had been the driving force behind hundreds of the historical markers[51] that now stand in Houston County and was beloved by many, the mayor at the time actually even declaring a day named in her honor.

When Bishop passed away, however, a cache of letters, papers and documents concerning the Slocum Massacre (including Dr. Hayes's marker request) was discovered at her home. She hadn't kept the massacre literature at the Historical Commission's office with the rest of the commission holdings. She kept it separate and hidden at her residence.[52]

CHAPTER 10

CONCLUSIONS

I

A British detective successfully trailed Dr. Crippen across the ocean and arrested him in Canada on a charge of murder. A Kentucky detective traveled 19,000 miles after Wendling[53] was accused of child murder, visiting in his search such distant points as Buffalo, Monterrey and Honolulu; he caught his man and Wendling must go to trial. Near Palestine, Texas, 20 negroes have been slaughtered within 48 hours by whites; a mob of several hundred white men has engaged in a man hunt, killing negroes wherever found. The sheriff expresses the opinion that practically all the negroes murdered were unarmed, harmless and peaceable. Says the sheriff: "Throughout that section white men have been going about killing negroes as fast as they could find them, and as far as I have been able to ascertain, without any real cause. These negroes have done no harm that I could discover. There was just a hot-headed gang hunting them down and killing them."

Whether the 200 or 300 members of this Texas mob prepare to put up a plan of self defense or insanity does not matter. They will never be arrested and they will never come to trial. Texas with one-twentieth the population of the United States has one-tenth of all the homicides; mobs and individuals kill without hindrance, and conviction and legal execution of white men for murder are practically unknown in this state.

After a transatlantic chase, Dr. H.H. Crippen was hanged in London for the murder of his wife. Some noted that it was preposterous that lawmen could apprehend criminals across continents and oceans but not down the road in Anderson County. *Fort Worth Record*, August 2, 1910.

> *It is a bad sort of advertising, and if the laws, the courts, and the juries cannot correct this deplorable situation, it rests with the people at large through general education and elevating of public sentiment to place the value of a human life above that of a vagrant dog.*
>
> —El Paso Herald, *August 1, 1910*

AN ACT OF GENOCIDE IN EAST TEXAS

In late July 1910, hundreds of armed white men started killing African Americans in the Slocum-Augusta area, reportedly any and as many as they could find. And this went on for a minimum of two days, after which only eight casualties were reported.

Considering the southeastern portion of Anderson County and the northeastern portion of Houston County were "thickly settled" with African Americans in 1910, one armed white man could easily have murdered eight black folks in a period of twenty-four to forty-eight hours, even if he was on foot and especially if his targets were unarmed and unsuspecting. Hundreds of armed white men would readily have dispatched dozens of African Americans (if not hundreds), even if the targets were in various stages of flight. The consensus among descendants of the Slocum Massacre victims is that hundreds died in the bloodshed, and this estimate is not unreasonable. In fact, the evidence plainly suggests it.

The county sheriff heading the investigations said that there were bodies scattered everywhere and the buzzards would find many of them first—but incredibly (and clearly suspiciously), no bodies were discovered after the initial official eight. African American families collected and privately interred an untold number of their loved ones' bodies themselves to spare them further abuse, while white executioners were no doubt sneaking back to crime scenes and burying or destroying incriminating evidence. Newspaper accounts noted that black citizens were mistakenly shot when they panicked at the sight of white law enforcement officers, but none of these victims was ever identified. The district judge essentially threw up his hands and admitted to focusing on bringing the guilty to justice rather than determining how many victims were involved—because there was no way to make that determination. And three separate massacre narratives mention unmarked mass graves.

The truth is, a harrowing number of African Americans were slaughtered in the counties of Anderson and Houston in the mid-summer of 1910, easily eclipsing the body count of the Rosewood Massacre in Florida and surely surpassing that of the Tulsa Riots in Oklahoma, probably establishing the Slocum Massacre as the single, largest pogrom of blacks in modern American history.

And yet today it's almost never spoke of, much less widely acknowledged, sufficiently researched or historically considered.

II

Among the other reports as to the cause of the riot is that some time ago, one of the negroes wrote a letter saying that within a week he would have a white wife…

—Dallas Morning News, *August 1, 1910*

Regarding the Slocum Massacre, we now have a better sense of *who, what, where, when* and *how,* but the *why* is somewhat elusive. Contemporary newspapers all listed a disputed debt between a white man and a black man or a white citizen offended by a black county road repair summoner as potential impetuses for the massacre, or a combination of the two.

The debt dispute motive was introduced by Reddin Alford, who in every contemporary report enjoys the relatively harmless classification of a wronged bystander. His complaint obviously plays an important role in the affair, especially if it was amplified ulteriorly, but what is missed in most accounts (and neglected in the one report it appears in)[54] is his possible role as agitator.

In the August 2 edition of the *Dallas Morning News,* Deputy Sheriff Stubblefield mentions that Alford informed him that Abe Wilson had been plowing his fields with a shotgun attached to his plow and had told a local preacher that "if all white people were upon the brink of hell, he would help push them all in."

Alford undermines Wilson after having already incriminated Marsh Holley in the debt dispute, which Holley himself suggested was a trivial affair. And Alford's disparagement of Wilson might have been as contrived as the alleged debt dispute (especially when one considers Wilson and Holley were in-laws—Abe's wife, Ava, was a Holley). Abe (or "Old Abe" as he was called) Wilson[55] was a prominent figure in the local African American community and respected by at least enough local white citizens to be tasked with announcing the forthcoming road maintenance effort the county was trying to organize. He owned and operated a family store that was patronized by black and white residents alike and didn't seem like a man prone to flippant or cryptic comments about white people, especially not to or around white people.

It begins to appear that Alford[56] might have been something of a troublemaker himself, but even if he was, it might not get us much closer to discerning the real motive behind the massacre.

Jerry Sadler and his family believed it was a thinly veiled land grab. The Wilson and Holley families were both considerably propertied, and Alford's specific, perhaps calculated disparagement of prominent members of both these families supports the "land grab" viewpoint. Dr. Granville J. Hayes implied the massacre was an act of genocide based on racial hatred, his correspondence with Eliza Bishop resembling John A. Siddon's letter to Cecil Lyon. There was plenty of racial enmity in the region, and it clearly could have been exacerbated by the conspicuous prosperity of the Wilson and Holley families. But what if the Slocum Massacre was incited by neither a debt dispute nor an insulting summons?

A preponderant number of African American lynchings in Texas (and elsewhere) involved white women. Even looking at white women could get a black man lynched in America, and it is certain that few black men in East Texas would have risked such action in the early twentieth century, but it did occasionally happen. The lynching of an eighteen-year-old African American named Ted Smith in Greenville on July 28, 1908, is one example.

The sanctity of white women wasn't just an excuse for lynching in the South. On June 14, 1920, six African American circus workers were arrested for the alleged rape of a white woman in Duluth, Minnesota. On June 15, a white mob seized Elias Clayton, Elmer Jackson and Issac McGhie and hanged them. *Courtesy of Wikimedia Commons.*

THE 1910 SLOCUM MASSACRE

Ted Smith and his kin worked as laborers for the Delancey family on their farm just outside Greenville, in Hunt County. According to oral accounts, a relationship sprang up between Smith and fifteen-year-old Viola Delancey, and they carried on in secret. When Viola's parents caught on, they had Smith arrested. When Smith was later brought before Viola to be identified as an assailant, she (under pressure from her family) said, "That is the nigger that did the deed." Smith cried out in shock and was dragged to the town square by a rope around his neck. There, the mob doused him in oil and burned him at the stake in front of one thousand people.

Viola later recanted, and the county sheriff eventually admitted that Smith had been innocent. No one involved in the lynching was ever charged or prosecuted, and two of the lynch mob ringleaders would later rise to the public offices of Hunt County sheriff and Greenville fire chief.

There was no specific evidence that compelled me to pursue the "black man disrespects/assaults (or otherwise molests) the exalted southern white female" angle (the most loathsome cliché in the history of American lynching) in the events leading up to the Slocum Massacre, but something in the 1910 census caught my attention, and it turned me toward other considerations.

As mentioned in Chapter 1, after Lusk Holley was shot and lay quietly (pretending to be dead until his assailants passed), a second group of white men came through, and Jeff Wise lamented the Holley brothers' murders. I recorded this mention as an interesting anecdote but reconsidered it when I examined Sheet 5B of Enumeration District No. 16 of the 1910 U.S. Census for Precinct 3 of Anderson County. Line ninety listed Melvin Wise as the head of a household that included Jefferson (Jeff) Davis Wise; his wife, Lucy; his aunt Katie; and two "hired" men, John H. Hays and Cleve Larkin. Larkin was the first officially recorded casualty of the massacre; Hays was the only officially recorded solo casualty. For them to have been listed in the Wise household (which meant only that they resided on the Wise property, not in the actual house), they would presumably have to have been steady, reliable and, to some extent, trusted hands. And yet there was no reported complaint or outcry from the Wise family when members of their extended household—the only two servants they listed in the 1910 census—were slain. And there was no effort to spare Hays's or Larkin's remains a mass burial (if, as assumed, one or both were interred at the mass grave at Dick Wilson's place).

A few pages back in the 1910 census, Sheet 3B of Enumeration District 16, also jumped out at me. Line sixty listed Jim Spurger as the head of a household that included his wife; his sixteen-year-old daughter, Hattie M.; his fourteen-year-old daughter, Mattie; his nine-year-old daughter, Addie;

his eight-year-old daughter, Annie; his four-year-old daughter, Zadie; and his one-year-old son, Buford. One country door down from the Spurger household was the Holly Burley residence, kin of reported Houston County victim Will Burley (and the family whose rapid exodus was detailed in Chapter 6). Two doors down from the Spurger household (line fifty-five), Willie Foreman was listed as a "hired man" for the Jack Holley household (line forty-eight, page 3A), a black family, Jack being the father of Lusk (who also resided in that household) and the owner of a significant amount of land and a local store. And four doors away was the property of Abe Wilson (line thirty-seven, page 3A), himself a storeowner and county road maintenance summoner, father of injured Charlie W. Wilson and possible relative of victims Dick and Jeff Wilson, murdered over by the Percilla and Grapeland Road.

Cleve Larkin, John H. Hays and Willie Foreman were all hired men in the area. Larkin, Hayes, Foreman, the Holley brothers and Charlie Wilson were all acquaintances if not friends, and they had something else in common: they were all single. They were young, single black men passing in and out of an area just down the way from an extremely racist white man who had a house full of white daughters, at least two of whom were close to marrying age.

Alex Holley was an African American youth of bright complexion whose own family conceded was known to flirt with white women.[57] What if Alex Holley or John H. Hays (or Will Burley) had flirted with or made advances toward (or gave someone the impression of having flirted with or made advances toward) one of Spurger's daughters? What might a man like Spurger do? Would he stop at the black transgressor(s) alone? Or would he kill the lot to make sure word of his daughter's possible forbidden association or indiscretion never got out?

It is speculation only, but this scenario or one akin to it could explain why the Wise family never appeared to speak up or out about their hired men being shot down in cold blood. This could also explain why no one was ever charged in the murders of Alex Holley or John H. Hays. Miscegenation in that period and place would have been considered an abomination by average white folks, and even less radical or less racist white men would probably have closed ranks with a miscreant like Spurger to prevent interracial "contamination."

African Americans might have been frustrated or infuriated by the lynching of Leonard Johnson; there might have been a debt dispute, a county summons faux pas or a cryptic snipe. And blacks might have been emboldened by the outcome of the Johnson-Jeffries fight. Any of these potential catalysts could have evolved into a lynching (although none resembled the rationale for any of the other lynchings in East Texas over the last year or so), but were they compelling enough to initiate an act of ethnic cleansing or expulsion?

What if frustrations over a debt dispute, a county summons faux pas or a cryptic snipe, all perhaps pardonable, were compounded by a young African American male ogling or flirting (or mistakenly being perceived as ogling or flirting) with a young white woman like, for instance, one of Jim Spurger's two older daughters? What if a prospective lynching in the initial vein of Ted Smith's evolved into an Allen Brooks incident, where the white participants decided to keep going, or a scenario reminiscent of the 1886 Comanche County racial expulsion, where one lynching emboldened a racist element to tell the entire African American population to vacate the area posthaste, not-so-coincidentally allowing the remaining Caucasian elements to seize vacated lands and properties?[58]

Regardless of the impetus, what followed was an act of genocide that went unprosecuted, unpunished and unresolved and remains so to this day.

III

The continued existence of the colored prejudice that is peculiar to the American people is one of the most singular features of our national life. It is probably due to the lurking consciousness that the white people of the United States owe a debt to the Negro race that can never be repaid. None are so unforgiving as those who are conscious that they have most to be forgiven. It takes more than common magnanimity to cherish a friendly feeling toward those you have wronged, and the American people have hardly attained to that point of magnanimity yet. But we will get there in time, and learn to value men for their own qualities and not on account of their color or their pedigree.

—New York Age, October 13, 1910

On March 30, 2011, after a two-part February feature on the Slocum Massacre by Tim Madigan in the *Fort Worth Star Telegram*, the Eighty-Second Texas Legislature adopted House of Representatives Resolution 865 (HR 865—filed by Representatives Marc Veasey[59] and Lon Burnam[60] on March 11), acknowledging the incident:

AN ACT OF GENOCIDE IN EAST TEXAS

RESOLUTION:

WHEREAS, The year 2010 marked the centennial of the Slocum massacre, a horrific incident in our state's history and one that is deserving of attention and discussion; and

WHEREAS In the summer of 1910, racial tensions were running high in East Texas after the lynching of an African American in Cherokee County and the subsequent rumors of unrest among area blacks; in the small community of Slocum, in Anderson County the atmosphere grew more heated when a dispute arose between an African American resident and a white man over an unpaid debt; around the same time, several whites in the area had become incensed over what they viewed as inappropriate behavior by certain blacks; in late July, these factors combined to touch off a violent and deadly attack; and

WHEREAS, A mob of white men brandishing rifles, shotguns, and pistols descended on Slocum and began firing on unarmed African Americans; the attackers were estimated to number as many as 1,000 people, and their bloody rampage took a heavy toll; the murder of eight people was confirmed, and reports indicated that many more may have died in what became known as the Slocum massacre;

WHEREAS, The incident was reported in newspapers across the nation, and Texas Rangers and state militia were sent to the area to prevent further bloodshed; an investigation by an Anderson County grand jury overseen by Judge B.H. Gardner of Palestine led to the indictment of seven people, including Jim Spurger, who was believed to have been the prime instigator in the attacks; because of the emotions surrounding the case, Judge Gardner moved the trial to Harris County, but it was there that the wheels of justice stopped turning; the prosecuting attorney never brought the case to trial, and no one was ever convicted of the crimes; and

WHEREAS, In Slocum the African American survivors mourned their lost friends and loved ones and lived in fear of further violence; ultimately, many of them chose to move away, abandoning homes, stores, and farms; ancestors of the Hollie family suffered the loss of one son and the wounding of another, and they were forced to abandon property that included a home, a store, and several hundred acres of farmland; and

WHEREAS, The event wreaked devastation in the lives of African Americans living in the area, yet it has since been largely ignored, receiving no formal acknowledgement by state or local officials and little coverage in historical accounts of the era; and

WHEREAS, Only by shining a light on previous injustices can we learn from them and move toward a future of greater healing and reconciliation; now, therefore, be it

Statue of John H. Reagan in Reagan Park. Like his statue, Reagan cast a long shadow (especially over Palestine and Anderson County). *Author's collection.*

RESOLVED, *That the House of Representatives on the 82nd Texas Legislature hereby acknowledge the Slocum massacre of 1910.*

Veasey
Burnam

Ultimately, HR 865 was a nice official gesture, but it concluded with an ineffectual platitude observing that "only by shining a light on previous injustices can we learn from them and move toward a future of greater healing and reconciliation." Acknowledgement is an important step, but a meaningful commitment toward resolution would have been more useful and appropriate than a political courtesy.

The Texas legislature needed to appoint an investigatory committee to research the massacre comprehensively, interviewing descendants and family members, locating mass graves, examining property records and conducting archaeological studies, exhumations, DNA research, et cetera.

HR 865 was incurious when it needed to be inquisitive. And it was also oddly myopic, mentioning only one family affected by the massacre when there were dozens—the Barnetts, the Burleys, the Larkins, the Piersons and the Wilsons, to name a few.

IV

Here was our problem after the war:

A hostile government at Washington. A disreputable one at home. Heavy taxes; everybody poor; no money in the country; labor conditions completely upset; half the population (the negroes) refusing to work; resistance of the whites almost, if not completely broken and hope about gone. And then a ray of light out of the darkness. Some southern mind had conceived an idea pregnant with possibilities. Every southern man and woman knew of the superstitious mind of the negro, but one conceived the idea of using that superstitious mind to lead us out of the morass of evil into which our circumstances had thrown us. The KU KLUX KLAN was born. It was the savior from evil and oppression that nothing else could have lifted us so easily and completely in so short a time.[61]

—Charles H. Moore Reminiscences, 1932–33, *Briscoe Center for American History, University of Texas–Austin*

The machinations that John H. Reagan recommended to reestablish and maintain "good [Anglo] government" and the "repose of [white] society in Anderson County" were remarkably effective and it should come as no surprise that they were supplemented by the terrorist methods of the Ku Klux Klan and, in its absence, the racist ilk at the center of the Slocum

Massacre. Moore was referring to the first incarnation of Klan, which lasted from 1865 to 1874, but the Klan reappeared a few years after the Slocum Massacre.

According to Jerry Sadler, his father and the Barnett family might have sent one of the last of the white mobs packing at or near the end of the bloodshed, but it was not the last they heard from them:

> *That was the end of the massacre, but not the end of Papa's trouble with what became, about two years later, a reorganized Ku Klux Klan…*
>
> *If the experience taught the white leaders anything, it was to be wary of Papa and to tread carefully over matters of law. A few years after things cooled off, one of the leaders of the massacre tried to use the law itself to take the black Sadlers'[62] land from them…Papa came to their aid and hired lawyers who took the case all the way to the state supreme court, which upheld the negroes' right to the land.*
>
> *By this time, the Klan was an organized movement, hiding behind bedsheets on their night rides. They could not hide their identities from the negroes or from us, because we could always recognize the shoes, but most of the time they succeeded in hiding from the law. Because they couldn't be prosecuted for making threats or issuing warnings, they didn't hesitate to appear in the daytime without their covering. That was the case in 1925 when six prominent men rode up to our house in a shiny new car to warn Papa.[63] "There might be some trouble if you have any niggers living on the place."*
>
> *One would have thought that these men would've learned eventually that their threats succeeded only in stirring up Papa's hot temper, but they never seemed to learn. After I was grown and out on my own, I was called home time after time to help defend the homestead because the Klan was stirring up trouble…*

The second incarnation of the Klan in the area remained a force until the early to mid-1940s, and then it was back to the John H. Reagan script.

When the Civil Rights Act of 1964 and the Voting Rights Act of 1965 were passed, the Anderson County Commissioner's Court began devising new ways to *less enfranchise* if they could no longer *disenfranchise* African American citizens.

In 1969, commissioners reapportioned the county precincts to dilute the black vote, and three local black citizens, Frank J. Robinson,[64] Timothy Smith and Rodney Howard, fought back. They studied up, secured financial backing (from the AFL-CIO and the A. Philip Randolph Institute) and received legal representation from the American Civil Liberties Union (ACLU).

In 1973, with Robinson as the lead plaintiff, the trio of African Americans filed suit against the Anderson County Commissioner's Court in Eastern District Federal Court in Tyler.

On March 5, 1974, they received a hearing from district court judge William J. Justice, and on March 15, Judge Justice concluded that the reapportioned districts were a result of racially motivated gerrymandering and ruled in favor of Robinson, Smith and Howard.

When the Anderson County commissioners appealed the ruling to the Fifth Circuit U.S. Court of Appeals, circuit court judge Irving Goldberg confirmed the findings of the Eastern District Federal Court, expressing "profound disappointment in the irresponsibility" of the Anderson County Commissioner's Court and concluding that it "cut the county's black community into three illogical parts in order to dilute the black vote in precinct elections, acting as a modern Caesar dissecting its private Gaul."

The verdicts resulted in a significant challenge to a century of blatantly racist politics in Anderson County, with black leaders soon representing black constituencies in virtually every area of local government, from the justices of the peace to the city councils and school boards. The progress spread to the surrounding counties, and Robinson, Smith and Howard subsequently liberated the entire political landscape of East Texas.

In 1976, Robinson filed a second suit to require Palestine city commissioners to be elected from individual districts and created the East Texas Project to organize and advocate for similar litigation in other East Texas communities.

On October 13, 1976, however, Robinson was mysteriously killed by a single gunshot wound to the head in his garage at his home in Palestine. Local authorities ruled the seventy-four-year-old's death a suicide despite the obvious suspicious timing of the incident and purported evidence contrary to the findings.[65]

Robinson's shotgun had been fired at least twice, once into a garage wall, and three spent shell casings were found on the scene. Robinson's widow claimed she had never seen him in their garage with the gun and questioned the assumption that he would ever go there with a firearm. Others suggested that a hired assassin was brought in from the outside to kill Robinson and snuff out his ongoing and future civil rights efforts.

Dr. John Warfield, a University of Texas professor and secretary of the National Black Political Assembly, was unequivocal. "It is clear that this Ku Klux Klan–style of murder and terror is as real on the 200th anniversary of this

Wood engraving depicting an African American family "visited" by the Ku Klux Klan, published in *Harper's Weekly* in 1872. White Anderson County residents embraced the Klan during Reconstruction and after the Slocum Massacre. *Courtesy of Library of Congress.*

immature nation as it was in the 19th century," he said. "There is a conspiracy in this state to obstruct the political rights and political awakening of black and brown people and the powerful potential constituency they represent."

On Tuesday, October 19, Warfield noted that black people in Palestine "have little faith in the police department" because "they are not prone to provide justice for black people."[66]

"There had been no recent controversy or threat," Warfield added, "but the people there just feel [Robinson] was too aggressive…I guess he just wasn't getting old fast enough for the people in that area."

In 1994, the Texas Civil Rights Project sent researchers into the city of Palestine to study the relationship between local law enforcement agencies and the minority population of the community. The findings were consistent with local historical trends:

> *Officers of the Palestine Police Department and Anderson County Sheriff's Deputies routinely engage in discriminatory and abusive practices, creating a racially and ethnically biased environment of law enforcement in Palestine.*
>
> *As a result, Hispanics and African Americans suffer an inordinate number of false arrests, excessively high bail for misdemeanor or non-violent charges, and detentions for months in cases in which no formal misdemeanor charges or felony indictments are ever filed.*
>
> *Furthermore, police and sheriff's officers routinely stop, ticket, and illegally harass Hispanics and African Americans as they try to go about their daily lives.*
>
> *Law enforcement agents summarily arrest, and even detain, African American and Hispanic individuals for offenses that generally merit a field release citation.*
>
> *The threat of police harassment and the inherent unfairness within the courts in Palestine and Anderson County pervades the day-to-day lives of resident Hispanics and African Americans.*[67]

V

Racial violence erupted in the small and quiet Rosewood community January 1–7, 1923. Rosewood, a predominantly colored community, was home to the Bradley, Carrier, Carter, Goins, and Hall families, among others. Residents supported a school taught by Mahulda "Gussie" Brown Carrier, three churches, and a Masonic lodge. Many of them owned their homes, some were business owners, and others worked in nearby Sumner and at the Cummer Lumber Mill. This quiet life came to an end on January 1, 1923, when a white Sumner woman accused a black man of assaulting her. In the search for her alleged attacker, whites terrorized and killed Rosewood residents. In the days of fear and violence that followed, many Rosewood citizens sought refuge in the nearby woods. White merchant John M. Wright and other courageous whites sheltered some of the fleeing men, women and children. Whites burned Rosewood and looted livestock and property; two were killed while attacking a home. Five blacks also lost their lives: Sam Carter, who was tortured for information and shot to death on January 1; Sarah Carrier; Lexie Gordon; James Carrier; and Mingo Williams. Those who survived were forever scarred.

Haunted by what had happened, Rosewood residents took a vow of silence, lived in fear and never returned to claim their property. That silence was broken seventy-one years later. In 1994 survivors, including Minnie Lee Langley, Arnett Turner Goins, and Wilson Hall, filed a claims bill in the Florida Legislature. A Special Master, an expert appointed by the Speaker of the House, ruled that the state had a "moral obligation" to compensate survivors for the loss of property, violation of constitutional rights, and mental anguish. On May 4, 1994, Governor Lawton Chiles signed a $2.1 million compensation bill. Nine survivors received $150,000 each for mental anguish, and a state university scholarship fund was established for the families of Rosewood and their descendants. A fund was also established to compensate those Rosewood families who could demonstrate property loss.

—Text of the Rosewood Massacre Florida Heritage Marker (Levy County), sides one and two, dedicated by Governor Jeb Bush in May 2004

It might not be fitting to start the final section of a book on the Slocum Massacre with the text of the Rosewood Massacre's Florida Heritage Marker, but the two massacres have many similarities, and the State of Florida's eventual, earnest response to its parallel disgrace places Texas's shameful unresponsiveness (the toothless acknowledgement of HR 865 notwithstanding) in stark contrast.

THE 1910 SLOCUM MASSACRE

In 1994, while Anderson County law enforcement personnel were discriminating against folks of color, the decision in *Rosewood Victims v. the State of Florida* made the Sunshine State the first state to award victims and descendants of victims of racial violence compensation for their sufferings and losses. Two years later, the Oklahoma legislature commissioned a report to document the events of the Tulsa Riots, acknowledging the number of victims and the extent of the damages the black community there suffered. The commission's findings were released in 2001, and the State of Oklahoma responded with scholarships for descendants of survivors, funding for economic development at the site of the carnage and a memorial park dedicated to the victims of the riots.[68]

The Slocum Massacre—which, again, was worse than the Rosewood Massacre and likely surpassed the Tulsa Riots in terms of body count—has no memorial or historical marker, and the State of Texas has yet to muster the courage or political will to commission a full-scale investigation of the pogrom, much less consider possible recompense for the descendants of the massacre victims. The 1910 Slocum Massacre is just something white folks got away with back then and don't trouble themselves too much over today. Especially in Anderson County.

The city of Palestine is home to the Museum of East Texas Culture (adjacent to the John H. Reagan statue in Reagan Park), and it has a small first-floor room devoted to African American history in the region. The African American "room" contains no mention of the Slocum Massacre. Meanwhile, in April 2013, the City of Palestine opened a new Confederate Veterans' Memorial Park in the downtown area.

———

The community of Slocum itself performed a symbolic gesture (knowingly or unknowingly) a few years back.

According to some Slocum school graduates, if you grew up in Slocum and went to school there and played on the school playground, you played under the watchful gaze of the Hanging Tree, rumored to have been the spot where past Slocum citizens hanged African Americans. Some years it was even used as a backdrop for school pictures.

And then Slocum school officials paved the area, eventually cutting down the Hanging Tree. Today, there is nothing left except an unpaved spot near the edge of the parking lot.

Whether a matter of conscience or practical necessity, it was the right thing to do. It broke a terrible cycle.

Despite denials, selective memory or cultural amnesia, there is little doubt that the community of Slocum is aware of its frightful past and endeavors mightily to transcend it even while refusing to acknowledge it. But silence is not the proper course of action for Slocum or Anderson County or the State of Texas. The Slocum Massacre will not remain buried.

On some level, the State of Texas was complicit in an act of genocide. Malevolent forces in both Anderson County and Houston County covered up the actual act itself and continue to cover it up to this day. And past white residents of Slocum, Denson Springs and Percilla benefitted from the act of genocide, the resultant expulsion and the long-running coverup.

This outrage should be shameful to all Texans.

The atrocities committed in the Slocum area in 1910 should give us all pause and spur commitments to definitively establish the truth, fully acknowledge it and honestly and constructively address it.

We are less as a state and a people until we do.

NOTES

CHAPTER 1

1. The *Palestine Daily Herald* called him "Reddin Alford." The *Crockett Courier* called him "Alford Anderson." The *Fort Worth Record* referred to him as "Rexford Alford." This text will follow the *Daily Herald*'s nomenclature.

2. On December 23, 1897, an African American man named Jim Jones was cut on the head during a fight with one James Spurger in the Houston County city of Crockett. Jones was not seriously hurt, but Spurger was arrested and posted bond. It is likely that "James" and "Jim" Spurger are one and the same and that he had issues with his black neighbors for years.

3. Some members of the mob (and perhaps much of the white male population of Texas in general) felt cheated. The October 21, 1902 edition of the *Brownsville Daily Herald* was reassuring: "Jim Buchanan, the criminal thus executed, doubtless deserves a far worse fate than hanging, but his punishments were better left to the ruler of the lower region, where his soul, if he had one, must have gone instantly."

4. Ben Dancer might have been Dick Wilson's father-in-law. In the 1910 census (conducted in April), Wilson's mother-in-law, Courtney Dancer, is listed as a member of his household. After the massacre, she testified for the prosecution.

5. Dick Wilson was survived by his wife, Maggie, and his four sons and one daughter.

6. Mr. and Mrs. George Scarborough left southeastern Anderson County just over a month after the massacre. They moved to a farm east of Palestine.
7. Sam Baker was survived by his young wife, Lou, and his one-year-old-son, Arthur.
8. Byron Singletary later testified for the defense.

CHAPTER 2

9. Burrell Oaks was tried seven times for the killing of Sol Aronoff in Dallas on November 29, 1904—and found guilty six times. Whether the cases against him were solid or fair, his legal status epitomized the problems that critics of the Texas court system complained about.
10. Nine months after Leonard Johnson was hanged, shot and burned at the stake in Cherokee County, an African American named Anderson Ellis was burned at the stake in Rockwall. When local blacks attempted to thwart Ellis's lynching posse, a young black man named Will Clark was shot and killed.
11. Potiphar's wife attempted to seduce Joseph in Genesis 39.
12. The *Houston Chronicle* identified Mrs. Bailey as a newlywed and reported that she grappled with her Negro assailant and took the razor away from him.
13. Most of the black schools that did exist were underfunded and probably understaffed, giving whites an unfair advantage in terms of academic testing to earn suffrage.

CHAPTER 3

14. Reported in the July 31, 1910 edition of the *Fort Worth Star-Telegram*. The headline read, "Mob Pursues Negro, Intent on Violence." The subhead said, "Populace Inflamed by Story of Race Riot in East Texas Chases Black."
15. In this case, the *Chicago Defender*'s embellishment didn't lead to bloodshed. Nine years later, however, a *Defender* story initiated the Longview Race Riot of 1919.

CHAPTER 4

16. On July 28, 1908, the citizens of Greenville, Texas, burned an African American named Ted Smith at the stake in their town square. Greenville

was also infamous for a banner that hung over Lee Street (the main street in the downtown district) from the 1920s to the 1960s. It read, "Welcome to Greenville, The Blackest Land, The Whitest People." The motto also reportedly appeared on the city water tower.

17. There are no indications that any member of the all-white jury requested to be excused.

18. The August 4, 1910 edition of the *Houston Chronicle* referred to Judge Gardner's charge to the grand jury as a "masterpiece of its kind."

19. John A. Mobley was a state representative in the thirtieth and thirty-first legislatures. On January 12, 1909, he was even nominated for Speaker of the House of Representatives.

20. Judge Gardner probably knew Governor Thomas M. Campbell personally.

21. On September 30, 1910, not long after his work on the Slocum Massacre, Anders resigned and joined the Houston Police force.

CHAPTER 5

22. Preston and John A. Pierson were next-door neighbors. The closest white male resident would probably have been Henry C. Goff.

23. Unlike many of the refugees of the Slocum Massacre, Preston Pierson kept a copy of the deed to his land and retained possession of his property, selling it at a later date.

24. Preston Pierson passed away in Frankston on New Year's Day 1938. Estella Pierson passed away in Oakwood on March 3, 1950. Annie Pierson was found dead in her Frankston home on January 10, 1962. John A. Pierson died at Patton Hospital in Palestine on September 9, 1968. Elvie Ewell passed away in Frankston at the age of one hundred on April 4, 2004.

25. Dahomey was an African kingdom (in present-day Benin) that lasted from about 1600 until 1900. During the eighteenth and nineteenth centuries, it was a major hub for the Atlantic slave trade, providing approximately 20 percent of the slaves to Europe and the Americas.

26. A J.T. Killgo Cemetery can still be found off FM Road 2022 North near Slocum.

27. It is interesting to note that while Robert Killgo was part of one of the murderous mobs that marched through Anderson County killing African Americans in late July 1910, he had a "hired" black man named Noah Shamburger listed as a member of his household in the 1910

census (Anderson County Enumeration District No. 16, page 10B, line 76). Shamburger survived the hostilities and appears in the 1920 census (Anderson County Enumeration District No. 168, page 8B, line 90).

28. Turner E. Campe was also one of the original 350 men who founded the American Legion when its first meeting was held in Paris, France, on March 15, 1919 (*Kerrville Mountain Sun*, March 17, 1938).

29. Today, Lake Ioni is closed to the public. It and the land around it is part of the private Lake Ioni Fishing and Hunting Club.

30. 1920 Census, Anderson County Enumeration District No. 168, Sheet 6A, line 18.

31. 1920 Census, Anderson County Enumeration District No. 17, Sheet 2B, line 73.

32. 1920 Census, Anderson County Enumeration District No. 17, Sheet 2A, line 10.

33. *Palestine Daily Herald*, March 7, 1910.

CHAPTER 7

34. Aka Mac Reed, originally arrested for participating in the Slocum Massacre but never indicted and subsequently released.

35. One unidentified African American was lynched in Beaumont on February 2; another was lynched in Orange on June 6.

36. "I suppose we could have gone down there and killed him just as easy as the others." Here, Alvin Oliver—who was probably the unidentified suspect indicted with the others—frankly admits to some of the killings.

37. Alvin Oliver was alluding to the Leonard Johnson lynching, discussed in Chapter 2.

38. *Houston County Court Criminal Minutes*, Docket Book No. 6, p. 60.

39. Judge Gardner would go on to serve on the Texas Board of Legal Examiners from 1924 to 1938 and was considered the dean of East Texas lawyers at the time of his demise on April 13, 1947.

CHAPTER 8

40. The second, separate case against Jim Spurger was dismissed four months after the fire (see the reproduced Houston County Court Criminal Minutes in previous chapter). It is possible the second charge

was a prosecutorial gesture to keep Spurger, the clear Slocum Massacre ringleader, behind bars regardless of the larger case. It is also possible that the courthouse fire made the dismissal of the second charge unavoidable, securing Spurger's release if he was, in fact, still incarcerated.

41. O.M. Betsill was one of the guarantors of Henry Shipper's surety bond.

CHAPTER 9

42. W.T. Sadler (July 27, 1797–February 18, 1884) fought in the 1836 Battle of San Jacinto and was promoted to adjutant captain by General Sam Houston. Sadler could speak Spanish and was selected to interrogate General Antonio López de Santa Anna after his capture. Sadler was a representative to the Republic of Texas Congress (1844–45) and served in the first and second state legislatures after Texas was admitted to the Union.

43. In 1843, W.T. Sadler married again, this time to Permelia Bennett. Permelia and one of the Sadler children were killed by a tornado in 1866.

44. Despite the kindness and refuge Balis Madden and his relatives received from Patsy (or Betsy) and the other Edens slaves, he went on to fight for the Confederacy and died in Augusta on June 24, 1889.

45. Lusk Holley is buried in the Oakwood Cemetery. March Holley died nine months after Lusk (on December 16) and is buried in the Price Cemetery near Palestine.

46. Here Dr. Hayes is presumably recalling Andrew Kirkwood but confusing his first name with his last.

47. In Chapter 7, a reproduction of the Houston County Courthouse Criminal Minutes indicated a second charge against Jim Spurger, which wasn't resolved until April 19, 1913. If Spurger remained in jail until that charge was resolved (possibly by the courthouse fire), he might have (as Dr. Hayes recollected) been imprisoned for two and a half years.

48. The current Sand Flats Missionary Baptist Church is rumored to be sitting at the original Silver Creek School site.

49. Sometime after the Slocum Massacre, Dr. Hayes's father purchased some of the subsequently cheaper land around Denson Springs. J.W. and Granville Hayes appear there in the 1920 census (Anderson County Enumeration District No. 17, Sheet 4A).

50. According to one associate, Eliza Bishop exercised dictatorial control over what was deemed "history" in Houston County during her tenure as chairwoman of the historical commission.

51. One of the historical markers that came into being while Bishop was chairwoman of the Houston County Historical Commission was the marker for the Mary Allen Seminary, the first school for young black women in Texas.

52. Separate and hidden but not entirely inaccessible. In the early 1990s, Linda Sue Stuard, a student at the University of Texas at Tyler, wrote a paper on the Slocum Massacre (entitled "Racial Disorder in East Texas: The 1910 Slocum Incident"). It was the first relatively comprehensive piece of research ever composed on the subject (discovered tucked away in a folder in the Palestine Public Library). Stuard listed Bishop in her bibliography and noted examining some of the Dr. Hayes correspondence, which was "in the possession of Eliza H. Bishop."

CHAPTER 10

53. Joseph Wendling was a janitor convicted and sentenced to life in prison for the murder of nine-year-old Alma Kelmer in Louisville, Kentucky, in mid-December 1909. She was missing for six months before her remains were discovered on May 30, 1910.

54. *Dallas Morning News*, August 2, 1910.

55. After the massacre, Abe Wilson relocated to Freestone County and became a full-time farmer. He passed away in 1972.

56. Regardless (or perhaps because) of Reddin Alford's role in the Slocum Massacre, he went on to serve as president of the Slocum School Board in the 1920s.

57. In an interview with the *Fort Worth Star-Telegram* in February 2011, Jack Holley descendant Colecia Hollie-Williams (the Holleys changed the spelling of their surname from "Holley" to "Hollie" after the massacre because they were afraid of reprisals) said, "It would always be brought up in conversation. We'd be watching a movie or see something, or see an interracial couple, and they [her older family members] would say, 'Yeah, you remember Alex? He was killed for that.'"

58. Following the city of Comanche's lead, the Comanche County town of DeLeon (fifteen miles northeast) posted a sign over a well in the center of the community. It said, "Nigger—Don't let the sun set on your head in this town."

59. Marc Veasey is currently the United States representative for Texas's thirty-third congressional district, elected to that office in November 2012.

60. Lon Maxwell Burnam is the Texas state representative for House District 90, which encompasses downtown Fort Worth and surrounding areas.

61. Moore's views on this subject were commonly held. In *A Centennial History of Anderson County, Texas* (1936), Pauline Buck Hohes affirmed Moore's sentiments:

> *The cessation of hostilities did not end the South's distress. The negroes, liberated and given rights of citizenship were inclined to become a menace to civilization. Unlettered and their imagination fired with their new importance, to live amongst them promised to prove dangerous. The misguided sympathy felt for them by the Republicans led to measures being taken that were galling to the South and harmful to the negro himself. Martial law was declared...*
>
> *The "carpet baggers" and scalawags who swarmed into Texas after the war, organized the negroes into the "Loyal League." Meetings were held regularly where negroes were instructed as to their rights, etc. It grew hazardous at times for white women to walk the streets alone, negroes were so insolent and numerous. The menace of the situation forced the men of the South to take matters into their own hands. They organized the famous, "Ku Klux Klan." Today, after more than seventy years have passed, it is still felt that the step taken was necessary and wholesome for the negroes themselves. By its means the negroes were intimidated. They calmed down and behaved, and in time the new relations between ex-slave and former master adjusted themselves, and the two races found that they could live and work harmoniously in the same section without either harming or imposing on the other.*

62. There were some black Sadlers in the Slocum area, and the 1920 census indicates "Deaf and Dumb" Gus was working and living near them by then.

63. By the 1920 census, the Sadler family had moved to the Denson Springs area (Anderson County Enumeration District, page 17, Sheet 5B).

64. Robinson was a former educator and a retired superintendent of the Butler School system in Freestone County. Long after Abe Wilson migrated to this area, he would serve on the Butler School System Building Committee and work with Robinson.

65. Before an inquest ruled Robinson's death a suicide, even Texas attorney general Anthony Sadberry said, "I don't see where there can be evidence of a suicide beyond a reasonable doubt." After the inquest ruling, Sadberry backtracked and accepted the questionable pronouncement.

66. On November 20, 1976, a group identifying itself as the Anderson County Defense Fund offered a $2,000 reward "to anyone furnishing information leading to the capture, indictment and conviction of the person or persons responsible for the shotgun death of Frank J. Robinson." Timothy Smith, Robinson's associate in the gerrymandering suit against Anderson County, placed an ad announcing the reward in the *Palestine Daily Herald*. "There were too many unresolved questions concerning Robinson's death for the inquest verdict to be acceptable," Smith said.

67. From "Civil Rights in Texas—Eyes on Palestine: A Special Report to the Texas Civil Rights Project," August 1994 (excerpt from Part 1 of the Summary of Findings).

68. The Tulsa Race Riot Memorial Park was opened in 2010.

BIBLIOGRAPHY

Abilene Daily Reporter. "Grand Jury Will Probe Lynching." March 4, 1910.
———. "A Jail Delivery Causes Lynching." April 8, 1910.
———. "Judge Seay Will Order a Rigid Probe in Lynching." March 6, 1910.
———. "Race Riot at Slocum Results in Death of 23 Negroes, 4 Whites." July 31, 1910.
———. "Seven Are Indicted on Murder Charges." August 19, 1910.
———. "State Cannot Convict Them." May 14, 1909.
———. "Tyler Officers Will Prosecute." May 4, 1909.
Abilene Semi-Weekly Farm Reporter. "Three Arrests Today In Slocum Race Riot." August 9, 1910.
The Academy: A Weekly Review of Literature, Science & Art. "Lynching of Ted Smith." August 15, 1908.
Aldrich, Armistead Albert. *The History of Houston County, Texas.* San Antonio, TX: Naylor Company, 1943.
Alto Herald. "East Texas Race Riot, Several Are Killed." August 4, 1910.
———. "Negroes Lynched in Eastern Texas." May 7, 1909.
———. "Seven Men Indicted." August 25, 1910.
Arlington Journal. "Greenville Negro Burned." July 31, 1908.
Aspermont Star. "Dallas Lynching Ignored." April 14, 1910.
Austin American-Statesman. "Black Leader's Homicide Reported." October 15, 1976.
———. "Leave or Die: America's Hidden History of Racial Expulsions." July 9, 2006.

————. "Recalling the Fighting Champ of Texas Politics." January 26, 1990.

Beaird, J.L. "Letter to Dr. G.J. Hayes, October 26, 1984." Houston County Historical Commission.

Berry, Mary Frances. *Black Resistance/White law: A History of Constitutional Racism in America.* New York: Penguin Press, 1994.

Bishop, Eliza H. "Letter to Dan Utley, October 29, 1984." Houston County Historical Commission.

————. "Letter to Dr. G.J. Hayes, February 28, 1984." Houston County Historical Commission.

————. "Letter to Dr. G.J. Hayes, March 31, 1984." Houston County Historical Commission.

————. "Letter to Dr. G.J. Hayes, May 25, 1984." Houston County Historical Commission.

————. "Letter to Oliver B. McReynolds, October 29, 1984." Houston County Historical Commission.

Bonham Daily Favorite. "Texas Race Riots; 18 Negroes Killed." August 1, 1910.

Brownsville Daily Herald. "Excellent Example." October 21, 1902.

Bryan Daily Eagle and Pilot. "Anderson County Courthouse Burns." January 7, 1913.

————. "Can't Prove Anything." May 13, 1909.

————. "Frank Bates Lynched at Centerville." April 6, 1910.

————. "Local Option in Smith County." May 19, 1909.

————. "Names of Alleged Lynchers." May 6, 1909.

————. "Negro Killers Allowed Bail." May 11, 1911.

————. "Palestine Grand Jury Completes Its Work." August 19, 1910.

————. "Palestine Has Dedicated." September 10, 1910.

————. "Progress of Trial at Tyler." May 8, 1909.

————. "Ranger J.L. Anders Becomes Policeman." October 1, 1910.

————. "13 White Men Held in Jail." August 4, 1910.

————. "Wants Bail for Lynchers." August 3, 1910.

————. "Wants Bail for Lynchers." May 10, 1911.

————. "The Women of Tyler." May 15, 1909.

Bryan Morning Eagle. "Ravisher Soon Roasted." July 29, 1908.

Carpenter, John. *Memoirs of Benjamin Howard Gardner.* Briscoe Center for American History, TXC-ZZ Collection, 1944.

Charlotte News. "Slocum Resumes Its Normal Aspect." August 1, 1910.

Cherokee County Informer. "The Remnants of War." September 1998.

Chicago Defender. "200 Whites Killed and Many Wounded in Race War in Texas." August 6, 1910.

Chicago Inter-Ocean. "Score Killed in Race War; Towns Aflame." July 31, 1910.

The Crisis, November 1911. NAACP.

Commerce Journal. "East Texas Race Riot Several Are Killed." August 5, 1910.

———. "Turned to the Wall." August 5, 1910.

Corsicana Daily Sun. "Seven Killed and Score Injured in Palestine Storm." April 25, 1929.

Cravin, L. Arthalia. "Race Riots: Setting the Record Straight." *North Amarillo Now,* May 31, 2011.

Criminal Court Docket No. 6. *State of Texas v. Jim Spurger et al.* Houston County Courthouse Archives, October 14, 1910.

———. *State of Texas v. Jim Spurger et al.* Houston County Courthouse Archives, April 25, 1911.

Crockett Courier. "Arrested for Shooting." September 7, 1910.

———. "Eight Negroes Killed." July 31, 1910.

———. "Negroes Killed in Anderson County." August 7, 1910.

———. "Waived Examination." August 7, 1910.

Crosbyton Review. "Hold Lynchers Without Bail." May 20, 1909

Daily Bulletin (Brownwood). "Trembling Black Rushed onto Street and Hanged." August 1, 1910.

Daily Courier (Connelsville, PA). "Not Race War; Just Slaughter." August 1, 1910.

Dallas Morning News. "Anderson Quiet; Trouble Seems Over." August 1, 1910.

———. "Bail Asked in Slocum Case." May 4, 1911.

———. "Cutting at Crockett." December 24, 1897.

———. "Dallas Mob Hangs Negro from Pole at Elks' Arch." March 3, 1910.

———. "Defense of Lynching." August 12, 1903.

———. "East Texans Rally to Aid of Sufferers." April 26, 1929.

———. "East Texas Race Riot, Eighteen Negroes Killed." July 31, 1910.

———. "Further Details of Lynching." June 22, 1910.

———. "Grand Jury Takes Up Investigation." August 2, 1910.

———. "Hang Father; Son Spared." April 6, 1910.

———. "Johnson's Smiles His Main Work." July 5, 1910.

———. "Judges Who Dare to Perform Their Duty." June 3, 1909.

———. "Leveled by Storm, but Slocum Rises Again." June 21, 1936.

———. "The Lynching Habit in Texas." July 12, 1901.

———. "The Main Excuses of the Lynchers." March 4, 1910.

———. "Rehearing Denied Burrell Oats." October 17, 1912.

———. "Seven Indictments in Anderson County." August 18, 1910.

———. "Six Held Without Bail in Tyler Lynching Cases." June 1, 1909.

———. "Special Grand Jury to Probe Lynching." June 1, 1909.

BIBLIOGRAPHY

———. "Special Guard Withdrawn." March 5, 1910.

———. "Testimony For Defense in Tyler Lynching Case." May 13, 1909.

———. "Texas Jurist Passes Away." April 14, 1947.

———. "Two Worst Tornadoes in Texas History Killed 114 People." April 14, 1947.

———. "Tyler Lynching Cases Are Opened by Court." May 7, 1909.

Dallas Times Herald. "Palestine Stunned by Black Leader's Slaying." October 17, 1976.

Department of Justice. File No. 152961-1, R.G. 60, 1910.

———. File No. 152961-2, R.G. 60, 1910.

———. File No. 152961-3, R.G. 60, 1910.

Ellis, W.H. "Telegram to President Taft, August 1, 1910." Texas State Library and Archives.

El Paso Herald. "Arkansas Mob Lynches Negro." May 14, 1910.

———. "Has Souvenir Card of Dallas Lynching." March 7, 1910.

———. "Jail Breaker Hanged in Texas." April 9, 1910.

———. "Murder and Its Consequences." August 1, 1910.

———. "Murderous Mobs at Henderson, Texas, Fall Sullenly Back." October 16, 1902.

———. "Ten Negroes Are Killed in Texas Race Riots." July 30, 1910.

Evening Herald (Montpelier, IN). "Lust of Blood Actuated Mob." August 1, 1910.

Evening News (Ada, OK). "18 Killed in Race Riot." August 1, 1910.

Fort Worth Record. "Bloody Race War at Slocum: Eighteen Negroes Are Killed, No Fatalities Among Whites." July 31, 1910.

———. "Johnson Outclasses Big Jim Jeffries, Negro Is Victor in Fifteenth Round." July 5, 1910.

———. "Law Traps Dr. H.H. Crippen: Arrested On Board Steamer, Identification Is Complete." August 1, 1910.

———. "Negro Is Lynched by Posse of Whites South of Corsicana." July 6, 1910.

———. "Race War Ends, State Rangers Make Arrests." August 1, 1910.

———. "Slocum Riot To Be Probed By Grand Jury." August 2, 1910.

Fort Worth Star-Telegram. "Grand Jury Works on Riot Cases." August 3, 1910.

———. "Institutes Probe of Negro Killings." August 2, 1910.

———. "Mob Pursues Negro Intent on Violence." July 31, 1910.

———. "Negroes Guarded by State Troops Following Riots." July 31, 1910.

———. "Race War of Slocum Receives Resolution in Texas House." March 30, 2011.

———. "Seven at Palestine Face Murder Charge." August 18, 1910.

———. "16 Negroes, 4 Whites Killed in Texas Race Riots Near Palestine. July 30, 1910.

Fourteenth Census of the United States, 1920. Anderson County, Texas.

Galveston Daily News. "Continue Murder Cases." November 11, 1910.

———. "Gardner Delivered Grand Jury Charge." August 2, 1910.

———. "Hanged Till Dead." October 18, 1902.

———. "Landed at Rusk." October 17, 1902.

———. "Murdered a Girl; Burned at Stake." June 21, 1910.

———. "Victims of Slocum Mob Were Unarmed." August 1, 1910.

———. "Whites and Blacks Clash, Eighteen Negroes Killed." July 31, 1910.

Gardner, B.H. "Letter to Governor Campbell, August 4, 1910." Texas State Library and Archives.

General Assembly Resolution 260. "Convention on the Prevention and Punishment of the Crime of Genocide." United Nations General Assembly, December 9, 1948.

Grapeland Messenger. "Victims Were Unarmed." August 4, 1910.

Green, Felix. *The Piersons and Barnetts of East Texas.* N.p.: self-published, 2013.

Greenville Morning Herald. "Crime That Goes Unpunished." December 7, 1910.

———. "Race Riot: Bloodshed." July 31, 1910.

Grove, Larry. "Ugly Lynching Spoiled Dallas Aviation Debut." *Dallas Morning News,* May 6, 1963.

Harper's Weekly, February 24, 1872.

Harrison, Eric. "A Shadow of Doubt." *Fort Worth Star-Telegram,* June 20, 1982.

Hayes, Dr. G.J. "Letter to District Engineer, Texas Highway Dept., October 12, 1984." Houston County Historical Commission.

———. "Letter to Mr. Eliza H. Bishop, March 2, 1984." Houston County Historical Commission.

———. "Letter to Mr. Eliza H. Bishop, April 18, 1984." Houston County Historical Commission.

Hohes, Pauline Buck. *A Centennial History of Anderson County, Texas.* San Antonio, TX: Naylor Company, 1936.

Houston Chronicle. "Additional Arrests In Anderson County." August 1, 1910.

———. "Death and Bloodshed In Many Cities After Bout." July 5, 1910.

———. "Eastern Texas Race War Hot and Bloody. July 31, 1910.

———. "Fake Pictures Brought Riot." August 6, 1910.

———. "'I Couldn't Come Back, Boys,' Sighed Jeffries at Ring Side." July 5, 1910.

———. "Judge Gardner's Court Is Rushing Investigation." August 2, 1910.

———. "The Man Hunt Is Denounced." August 2, 1910.

BIBLIOGRAPHY

———. "Negro Lynched Near Corsicana." July 5, 1910.

———. "No Indictments Are Found in Palestine." August 15, 1910.

———. "Palestine Citizens Are Very Indignant." August 4, 1910.

———. "Palestine Grand Jury Recesses to Wednesday." August 7, 1910.

———. "Punishing the Guilty." August 4, 1910.

———. "Texas Hurt by Her Own People." August 18, 1910.

———. "13 White Men Held in Jail." August 3, 1910.

———. "21 Negroes Are Dead, 3 White Men Wounded." July 30, 1910.

Houston County Court Criminal Minutes Index. Houston County Courthouse Archives.

Houston Daily Post. "The South Needs Brave Judges." July 11, 1909.

———. "Troops Ordered Out." October 16, 1902.

Indianapolis Recorder. "New England Convention." June 7, 1913.

Jaspin, Elliott. *Buried in the Bitter Waters: The Hidden History of Racial Cleansing in America.* New York: Basic Books, 2007.

———. "Leave or Die: America's Hidden History of Racial Expulsions." *Austin American-Statesman,* July 6, 2006.

Jewish Herald. "The Press from All Over the Country." March 17, 1910.

Kennedy, Bud. "In Texas, History Is Still Battleground in Culture Wars." *Fort Worth Star-Telegram,* April 5, 2011.

Kennedy, Randall. *Nigger: The Strange Career of a Troublesome Word.* New York: Pantheon, 2002.

Knox County News. "Mob Lynches Black Criminal." March 11, 1910.

Logansport Pharos. "20 Negroes Killed by Texas Mob." August 1, 1910.

London Standard. "Negro Burned at Stake." June 22, 1910.

Los Angeles Herald. "Johnson Batters Jeff to Defeat in Fifteenth." July 5, 1910.

Lubbock Avalanche-Journal. "Blacks Ask Aid in Death Probe." October 19, 1976.

———. "Rights Leader Killing Called Conspiracy." October 20, 1976.

Lyon, Cecil A. "Letter to Hon. George W. Wickersham, August 15, 1910." National Archives and Records Administration.

Madigan, Tim. "A Century Later, Texas Race Massacre Forgotten by All but a Few." *Fort Worth Star-Telegram,* February 20, 2011.

———. "Story of Slocum Massacre of 1910 'Needs to be Told.'" *Fort Worth Star-Telegram,* February 27, 2011.

Mexia Weekly Herald. "Storm Takes Heavy Tolls in District." April 26, 1929.

Milford, G. "Letter to Thomas M. Campbell, Governor, Texas, August 2, 1910." Texas State Library and Archives.

Miller, Nathan. *Theodore Roosevelt: A Life.* New York: Harper Collins, 1993.

Minority Opportunity News. "Legacy that Bears the Scars of the Slocum Slaughter." July 1996.

Moore, Charles H. *"Reminiscences, 1932–1933."* Briscoe Center for American History Manuscripts.

NAACP. *Thirty Years of Lynching in the United States, 1889–1918.* Clark, NJ: Lawbook Exchange, 1919.

Nance, W.H. "Letter to Hon. Thomas M. Campbell, August 25, 1910." Texas State Library and Archives.

New York Times. "Because Innocent Persons." August 8, 1899.

————. "Calvary to Quell Outbreak in Texas." August 1, 1910.

————. "Fifty May Be Dead in Texas Race Riots." July 31, 1910.

————. "Jerry Sadler, Texas Politician Noted for Fights, Dies at 74." February 26, 1982.

————. "More Texas Riot Arrests." August 7, 1910.

————. "Scores of Negroes Killed by Whites." July 31, 1910.

————. "Texas Mob Lynches Negro in Jail Yard." August 3, 1920.

————. "Texas Mob Lynches Slayer." April 6, 1910.

————. "W.H. Ellis to Sue Texas." March 15, 1909.

Newark Daily Advocate. "Race Riot." August 1, 1910.

Ogdensburg Journal. "Troops to Stop Lynching." April 7, 1910.

Palestine Daily Herald. "Alleged Lynchers Released." July 9, 1909.

————. "All Quiet at Slocum." August 2, 1910.

————. "Burned at the Stake." March 8, 1909.

————. "Carried to Crockett." August 22, 1910.

————. "Convicts Were Seen." March 7, 1910.

————. "The County Commissioners." November 15, 1905.

————. "District Judge Seay of Dallas." March 8, 1910.

————. "Fewer Persons Slain by Mobs This Year." December 23, 1910.

————. "Grand Jury at Work." August 15, 1910.

————. "Grand Jury Recessed." August 6, 1910.

————. "Grand Jury to Resume" August 9, 1910.

————. "Judge Gardner on Mobs." July 10, 1909.

————. "The Legislature May Act." May 3, 1909.

————. "Negro Lynched at Tyler." May 1, 1909.

————. "Nine Are Bound Over." May 14, 1909.

————. "Prohibit Pictures." July 6, 1910.

————. "Rangers on the Scene." May 5, 1909.

————. "A Rapist Is Burned." June 21, 1910.

————. "Reported Trouble Is Not Confirmed." August 16, 1910.

————. "Reports Denounced By Palestine Citizens." August 3, 1910.

————. "To Resist Movement." July 7, 1910.

BIBLIOGRAPHY

———. "Seven Men Are Indicted on Charge of Murder." August 18, 1910.

———. "Situation in Hand, the Law Effective." August 1, 1910.

———. "16 Witnesses Heard." May 7, 1909.

———. "Three Men Liberated." August 13, 1910.

———. "Venue Is Changed to Harris County." December 14, 1910.

———. "Whites and Negroes in Serious Conflict." July 30, 1910.

———. "A Word of Warning." July 10, 1909.

Palestine Daily Visitor. "Court House Burns; Immense Conflagration. January 6, 1913.

Palestine Herald Press. "Circuit Court Affirms Ruling." December 26, 1974.

———. "Commissioners' Precincts Are Challenged in Federal Suit." November 30, 1973.

———. "County to Study Court Ruling." March 17, 1974.

———. "Hearing Set on Filing Motion." February 26, 1974.

———. "John A. Pierson." September 17, 1968.

Pettinos, Warren. Interview by author, October 13, 2013.

Pittson Gazette. "Seek Leaders in Massacre." August 1, 1910.

Poseyville News (Indiana). "Saved Negro He Wanted Hanged." February 18, 1910.

Proctor, Ben H. *Not Without Honor.* Austin: University of Texas Press, 1962.

Reagan, John H., with Walter McCaleb. *Memoirs, with Special Reference to Secession and the Civil War.* New York: Neale Publishing, 1906.

Record and Chronicle (Denton). "Would Denounce Tyler Lynchers." May 3, 1909.

Richards, Dave. *Once Upon a Time in Texas: A Liberal in the Lone Star State.* Austin: University of Texas Press, 2002.

Rogers, J.H. "Monthly Returns, Company C, Ranger Force, July 31, 1910." Texas State Library and Archives.

———. "Monthly Returns, Company C, Ranger Force, August 31, 1910." Texas State Library and Archives.

Rusk Cherokeean. "8th Victim of Slocum Tornado Dies." May 17, 1929.

Sadler, Jerry, and James Neyland. *Politics, Fat-Cats & Honey-Money Boys.* Santa Monica, CA: Roundtable Publishing, 1984.

San Antonio Light & Gazette. "James Gozey." May 14, 1910.

Semi-Weekly Courier-Times (Tyler, TX). "Galveston Negro Knocked Out Jeffries in Fifteenth Round." July 6, 1910.

———. "Grand Jury Begins Work on Negro Killing Cases." August 3, 1910.

———. "Mob Gets In Work Again." April 9, 1910.

———. "Race Riot Reported at Slocum, Anderson Co." July 31, 1910.

———. "The White Men Now Confined." August 13, 1910.

Session, Maxine. Interview by author, September 18, 2013.

BIBLIOGRAPHY

Shiner Gazette. "Hanging Too Good." October 22, 1902.

Siddon, John A. "Letter to Cecil A. Lyon, August 1, 1910." National Archives and Records Administration.

Southern Mercury. "Fixed for a Barbecue." October 16, 1902.

Southwestern Reporter. "Ex parte SPURGER et al." n.d.

State Herald (Mexia). "Tried and Hanged the Same Day." October 24, 1902.

Statesville Landmark (Statesville, NC). "Many Killed in a Texas Race Riot." August 2, 1910.

Stuard, Linda Sue. "Racial Disorder in East Texas: The 1910 Slocum Incident." University of Texas at Tyler, n.d.

Sunday Morning Herald (Amarillo). "Negro Lynched." May 15, 1910.

Swindle, Howard. "Civil Rights Leader's Widow Says Her Life Was Threatened." *Dallas Times Herald*, November 27, 1977.

Texas Civil Rights Project. "Civil Rights in Texas—Eyes on Palestine: A Special Report to the Texas Civil Rights Project." August 1994.

Texas Informer. "House Approves Slocum Massacre Resolution." April 2011.

Thirteenth Census of the United States, 1910. Anderson County, Texas.

Utley, Dan K. "Letter to Eliza H. Bishop, November 20, 1984." Houston County Historical Commission.

Waldron, J. Milton. "'Night Letter' to the Governor of Texas, August 1, 1910." Texas State Library and Archives.

Ward, James. "A Human Skeleton." Yale Center for British Art, n.d.

Washington Herald (Indiana). "Deaths Result from Race Riots." July 6, 1910.

———. "Fearful Toll in Texas Riot." August 1, 1910.

Washington Post. "Condemns Texas Slayers." August 8, 1910.

Weekly Democrat-Gazette (McKinney). "Burned Up Is the Black Fiend." July 30, 1908.

Wichita Falls Times. "$2,000 Reward Offered in Robinson Death Case." November 21, 1976.

Wickersham, George W. "Letter to Cecil A. Lyon, August 19, 1910." National Archives and Records Administration.

INDEX

INDEX

INDEX

INDEX

INDEX

INDEX

ABOUT THE AUTHOR

Born in Fort Worth and raised in Aledo, E.R. Bills has a degree in journalism from Texas State University. He lives with his family in north Texas and does freelance historical, editorial and travel writing for publications around his home state. He is also the author of *Texas Obscurities: Stories of the Peculiar, Exceptional and Nefarious* (History Press, 2013).

CPSIA information can be obtained
at www.ICGtesting.com
Printed in the USA
BVHW041925060220
571667BV00006B/29